Crossings:
A transpersonal approach

Crossings:
A transpersonal approach
Carl Levett

PUBLISHED BY
Quiet Song
Ridgefield Conn.

Library of Congress Catalogue Number 74-17597
International Standard Book Number 0-915054-01-9 (cloth)
0-915054-02-7 (paper)

Published by
Quiet Song
84 Riverside Drive
Ridgefield, Connecticut 06877

I would like to thank Ann Crawford, for her personal help and critical review; Julius, my father, for his faith; Bob Byars, for his insight and energy in editing the final draft; and Marge, my wife, for her affection and tender-loving-care through all my struggles.—C.L.

Names, locations, and all other identifying details have been carefully altered throughout this book to fully ensure the privacy of all concerned.

The quotation is from *The Voice of the Silence from The Book of the Golden Precepts,* translated and annotated by H.P.B. A Quest Book, published by the Theosophical Publishing House, Wheaton, Illinois 60187.

The poem is from *Alembic Quatrains* by Mac Gregory, 75-06 Woodside Avenue, Elmhurst, New York 11373.

Set in Linofilm Palatino by Black Dot, Inc.
Printed and bound by the Haddon Craftsmen.

Produced by Bob Byars and Bill Henkin

Designed by Lawrence Levy

Cover illustration by David Wilcox

To Lynn
Wayne
Paula
Jeanine

*The light from the one Master, the one unfading
golden light of Spirit, shoots its effulgent beams on
the disciple from the very first. Its rays thread through
the thick, dark clouds of matter.*
*Now here, now there, these rays illumine it, like sun-
sparks light the earth through the thick foliage of the
jungle growth. But, O Disciple, unless the flesh is
passive, head cool, the Soul as firm as pure as
flaming diamond, the radiance will not reach the
chamber, its sunlight will not warm the heart. . . .*

Crossings:
A transpersonal approach

Most people think of psychotherapists as a select group, and by conventional standards they are. The professional's unique status with its overtones of mystery and its lucrative income combine with the intimate nature of the doctor-patient relationship to create an air of specialness. The private practioner has additional advantages. He can select his patients by weeding out those who are incompatible with his lifestyle, temperament or philosophy, and adjust hours and fees in keeping with his self-image.

For many years I was a member of this unofficial club, concerned, as most professionals are, with being as helpful as I knew how to be. At home a variety of avocational interests such as sculpting, composing music, and building stone walls occupied my leisure time. Suburban Connecticut supplied a pastoral setting for harmonious living with my wife and teenage daughter.

Like most people, I had struggled with childhood conflicts that carried over into adolescence and early adulthood. But help from several competent clinicians had cleared away the main residue of inner distress, permitting me to explore new avenues of learning in my personal growth and development.

This was my life, prior to an event which caused a dramatic upheaval of my consciousness, shattered my long-held beliefs concerning psychotherapy, and, by its impact on my personal and professional life, set in motion the first of a series of crossings.

One day while driving I happened to notice a sign announcing weekly spiritual gatherings led by an East Indian Master. I often enter into situations impulsively and am also drawn to the esoteric, so at the appropriate hour I found myself at the door of an old, weather-beaten house.

Once we had removed our shoes, we newcomers were escorted upstairs to a quite ordinary room where a pleasant incense was burning. A small table covered with a clean white cloth held lighted candles and fresh-ly cut flowers. We joined those who were already seated and quietly awaited the Master's arrival.

He entered, a striking figure draped in a flowing, white, loosely cut garment, and assuming the lotus position closed his eyes and meditated for several minutes. A feeling of serenity slowly pervaded the room and it was in this calm that he opened his eyes and gave a short talk on conquering fear through the spiritual power of the heart. He spoke of human love; the quality of sacri-fice; and the disparity between the human personality and God-realization. His metaphors did not fit any of the concepts with which I was familiar, and although my skepticism kept me interested in his message I remained aloof to its import.

In the question-and-answer period that followed, he responded to all queries with patience and understanding, and, at the end of the evening, newcomers were brought to the front of the room. We knelt before him. His eyes conveyed a spiritual love which, together with his gestures, took the form of a blessing.

Stirred by this experience, I returned the following week, and this time at the end of the meeting the Master singled out several people, myself included, for special attention. He had us stand so that he could fix his eyes on each of us, and when he turned to me I was completely receptive. After a few moments my eyes fused with his and all my self-consciousness slipped away. I surrendered completely to the two powerful beams of light which flowed from his eyes and flooded my being with effulgence. Suddenly, a series of uncontrollable vibrations or electrical charges broke loose with a powerful force within me. It was as if a boulder had been flung into the center of a tranquil pond. It seemed as if this energy was trying to break free of my body. Unexpectedly, the Master's attention shifted away, breaking off the rapturous flow of energy between us. He smiled and silently acknowledged that our contact—which had seemed timeless— was now over. Although at the time the sensations that I felt had seemed to signal the beginning of a greater inner freedom for me, what followed was quite the opposite. A painful muscular constriction began to form in my abdomen.

In this unsettled state, I asked for a private conversation with the Master. Although his composure and sympathy put me somewhat at ease, I was worried about my steadily worsening abdominal tension. His only comment was, Don't concern yourself with that; just let the energy go. Not really satisfied with this advice,

I tried to question him further, but he merely repeated, Don't be concerned; just let it go.

The drive home was difficult since the constriction had become a spasm under my diaphragm, and its clamp-like pressure left me shortwinded. Despite my discomfort, I went to bed reassuring myself that after a good night's sleep the pain would be gone. But when I awoke the next morning my condition was worse.

My approach to personal problems in the past had been to submerge myself in the distress I was feeling without attempting to find an immediate solution. Years of experience had taught me there was a normal gestation period before awareness could deliver itself to problem-solving. I decided to wait it out and left ample time for reflection, but no awareness came. This surprised me, for my intuition had previously been quite reliable whenever I had faced a dilemma.

Even though I made sure not to impose any demands on myself that might induce further stress, the effects of impaired eating, breathing and sleeping left me little choice but to reconsider my original wait-and-see attitude. However, with a variety of professional techniques at my disposal, I felt certain that I could alleviate my indisposition.

For the next month I became both patient and therapist, drawing on such special approaches as bio-energetic, gestalt and primal therapy—disciplines considered by many people to be advanced in the treatment of body spasm. Although these same procedures had proven quite beneficial to many of my patients, they brought surprisingly little relief to me. I was completely baffled.

The thought occurred to me that perhaps I had been hypnotized, but I dismissed it after reviewing the training I had received in autosuggestion years before. My experience with the Master had little in common with what I had been taught. I finally concluded that I had been saturated with an amount of energy which had overwhelmed my nervous system in much the same way that excess current blows a fuse. In light of this, I turned to meditation and with little difficulty attained a state of calm leading to a generalized relaxation of my body. Yet my spastic condition remained unimproved.

Being run down physically was taking its toll on me. I thought my work inefficient and well below par, and considered taking a temporary leave from my practice. But the decision not to do so was made for me by my patients, who were helping themselves despite my withdrawn behavior. They were doing better as I was doing worse.

My wife was remarkably understanding and responsive to my difficulties. She cooked special foods at unusual hours without complaint although at times I barely ate at all, since almost everything I did eat led to days of indigestion. My sleep continued to be fitful.

As I revealed bits and pieces of my strange predicament to a few of my colleagues, hoping to gain some insight from them, I soon realized that they were unable to help. I was tempted to turn to our family doctor but decided to live with my anguish rather than be sedated with drugs. Throughout this entire period, I clung to the belief that there were homeostatic forces at work within me which would eventually restore my well-being, should all attempts at self-help fail. After weeks spent poring over medical, psychiatric and psychological publications, searching for any clue that might explain my symptom, I found useful only a brief passage which suggested that the process of self-realization sometimes produced symptoms of disturbance which were strikingly similar to those of a neurotic nature. My spirits were boosted by this suggestion, but only briefly.

Since the prospect of returning to the Master and becoming his disciple unsettled me, I discarded the idea, but I sensed nonetheless that I would continue to feel his presence. Just how, I wasn't sure. He had touched my deeper feelings, as one brother to another. I didn't want to break contact with him completely, so I wrote to him and explained that I was attempting to pursue the path of the heart on my own.

Submission had been alien to my temperament throughout my life, but the countless limitations of my condition had weakened my perceptions and rendered my life colorless and uninspiring. For the first time intuition, self-reliance and even my professional training had failed me. Face-to-face with helplessness, I was forced to admit I was stuck. Really stuck.

It was spring, and though many months had passed, my condition was unchanged. Consequently I spent my time, as most people would under similar circumstances, trying to find diversions from my problem. One day I wandered into a local music store and noticed a display of bongo drums. Although I had played several instruments over the years, my interest had never included percussion; but my attraction to the drums was unusually strong. I bought a typical pair of drums made from strips of wood with goatskin drumheads.

I was pleased with my purchase; too much time had elapsed since I had been good to myself. The prospect of having a new medium of expression—particularly one which might allow me to release some of my frustrations—was an enjoyable one.

Like a child with a new toy, I arrived home impatient to play. Although the instruction book explained how to hold the drums and how to move the fingers and hands to create tone variations, when I put the drums between my thighs and placed my hands as instructed, nothing happened. Suddenly I was uncommonly timid, not at all sure of the real nature of what I was attempting. Recalling the Master's words of advice, it occurred to me that letting go with the drums might also be the key to curing the spasm. Hesitantly; ever-so-lightly; I began to tap the drums.

I practiced each day, but had difficulty maintaining control. My hands would quickly tire and attempting to learn rhythms from the manual was restricting, so I tossed the book aside and decided to improvise instead. The drums and I remained strangers for some time. Yet when my hands occasionally expressed a greater freedom and flow, the drums responded with a more vibrant tone. With the exception of these encouraging moments, steady practice produced little that was inspiring. Then one evening I was able to watch and hear the bongos played by professionals. The dexterous, fluid movements of their hands amazed me, as did their ability to sustain a rhythm for long periods of time. When I tried to duplicate their rhythms, my efforts quickly broke down. But despite the poor results, I kept practicing in my own way.

Weeks later, while I was deep in thought during a practice session, my hands began to tap out a rhythm that caught my attention; it felt very personal, as if it belonged to me. I studied the pattern carefully and, concerned that I might forget it, recorded it on tape. When I played it back the following day, the beat sounded more intriguing than ever.

For several weeks I concentrated on sustaining this new beat—which required not thinking about my hands. In addition I found that if stray thoughts entered my consciousness, my hands stiffened, causing the rhythm to collapse, I experimented with reconciling these two difficulties and soon arrived at a solution: I focussed my concentration on an imaginary line running between the two drumheads. This permitted me to semi-observe the movements of my hands without consciously meddling. After overcoming initial periods of drowsiness, I was able to sustain the beat consistently for as long as five minutes without faltering. It was now fun to sit back, close my eyes, and turn my hands over to the drumming.

But one day while practicing I was shocked by the sudden realization that the drumming was coming not from me, but from somewhere else. I double-checked in disbelief, but it was a fact. The drumming continued in perfect rhythm, yet completely out of my control. Immediately my body began to convulse and energy surged from deep within me, becoming a liquid radiance which saturated every cell of my body. All conceptions I had of myself vanished as I dissolved into this flow. Suddenly I realized that the spasm had disappeared. A voice inside me was yelling *No more pain! It's gone! You've licked it!*

As the drumbeat became wilder, my meddling intellect kept trying to tell me this was impossible, even though it was clear my hands were plugged into an endless, absolute stream of energy. I knew this, not through logic or from past experience, but as pure feeling, convincingly real. *It* was drumming, and it was incredible— an all-knowing, ever-present and inviolable force. I felt no apprehension, only total submission. The beat became more subdued as the energy ebbed briefly, but it soon began to build again and gradually turned, moving back toward my center. I sensed what was to come and knew that I was powerless to stop it: the spasm was beginning to reappear. My brief experience of being dissolved in the flow was over. As the clamp closed around my gut, my only thought was *No! Please, God, no!*

The drumming had stopped.

My immediate reaction to this event was one of bewilderment. The thought of being at the mercy of a power beyond my personal control was frustrating, and my neatly arranged ideas were in disarray. I now knew there was a part of myself which was capable of cutting me off from the energy flow which was apparently my only means of resolving the spasm. I felt that same part of myself again intruding, reminding me of past successes and the challenges I had surmounted; I hesitated, sensing that any reliance on that aspect of myself would set off yet another round of resistance. Still, I had no choice but to let that awesome force control my hands again. Having briefly cleared my body of the spasm, I felt I could repeat the experience and by so doing learn how to lose myself in, and stay with, the flow.

But the next practice session was a fiasco. When I attempted to let my hands be taken over, tugging and grabbing sensations quickly interfered. It became obvious that the disruptions were the work of my structured-self, determined to maintain preeminence.

Changing my approach, I decided to let the left drum represent the coping, self-sufficient structured-me and the right drum the boundless, infinite, formless flow. This time, however, instead of keeping my attention riveted to the space between the drumheads, I allowed my consciousness to be slowly drawn toward the right drum, to find union with the outbound, transpersonal power. Each drumming foray brought the same result: increased mental turbulence. Structured-me quickly voiced its disapproval inside my head.

Think about your career, your reputation, your position in the community. What are you trying to prove?

It drew on my values, beliefs and cherished convictions.

Don't you know when you're well off? Look how hard you've struggled to establish yourself. You're on the inside now. Are you going to throw all that away for some kind of craziness?

Identity of self and feelings of alienation were problems I had worked on, and seemingly worked through, years before. My efforts had secured what I thought of as my real self, the true me.

Next came the plea of a despairing parent.

What will become of you . . . losing family and friends, leading a wasted life, disgracing yourself and everyone who loves you? That's the way it generally starts. First it's this non-sense, and then it'll be drugs and even worse.

I wondered how the hell drugs got into it as the unsolicited advice kept pouring in.

If you're so bored, take a vacation. Take up golf.

Then the voice became my accountant.

You've still got to make ends meet, you know. What about your expenses—the mortgage, the taxes, the insurance?

There was no denying that my structured-self had served me well over the years, helping me to establish a niche for myself in a generally inhospitable world, but listening to all this doomsday programming made me realize more clearly how frightened my structured-self was of my spirit's ascendence.

I pursued my drumming regimen with increased vigor, determined to strip away any remaining bindings and expose myself to the flow that I couldn't even identify, except in vague generalities.

For two weeks nothing significant happened, but then one night I was jolted from bed by a nightmare. In an overgrown, serpentine jungle, a fire was blazing under a huge pumpkin. Daimonic aboriginals danced orgiastically around the flames, wielding knobby clubs. Through the smoke I caught a glimpse of a body impaled on a spear. I realized with shock that it was me. This bone-chilling vision caused me to reflect more soberly. Until that time, I had assumed that surrender to the unknown force would be beneficent. My assurance wavered, but the attraction to that ethereal source which had invaded my psyche and demonstrated its strange powers of effecting relief as well as pain was now too important for me to disregard. My impulse to experience this unknown force more fully involved a desire to discover more of life's meaning, and so compelled me to search for more of the truth.

Although my newfound spirit flow seemed to be in mortal conflict with my structured-self, I was determined to pursue the issue. The basic concern became how to disintegrate structured-me. Returning to my drums, I had a sudden insight. Perhaps I could overload my nervous system, much as the Master had, but by using sound energy. Yielding to the sound waves was difficult; my body was unprepared. As I persisted, the pulsing drumbeat broke through, pressing itself tightly against the spasm. At first it was possible to tolerate this new pressure, but as it continued to increase, the discomfort proved too much to bear. I managed to redirect the power away from that pressure point and to disperse it as well. I was obviously on the right track, for as the energy intake increased tingling and shivering sensations began to careen through me. Shock waves surged through my nostrils, mouth, ears, eyes and genitalia—eventually even through the pores of my skin—pushing, shoving their way through myriad internal crevices, prodding my stiff muscles and joints into spontaneous and illogical movement.

Images began to appear like slides as compensation for my lack of total release—pictures of leaping, hurdling, racing down rapids; sunburst motifs, and roman candle explosions of blossoming spinoffs in sparkling colors; my being pulverized into tiny golden nuggets parading in long columns.

I felt my body yearning for greater freedom in a way that was reminiscent of the moment of suspension just before orgasmic release. The room echoed with sounds of my groaning, sighing, whimpering as my torso rose and fell in unison with the drumming. Suddenly, a plungerlike force attached itself to the spasm—creating a suction which pulled and yanked to set it free.

Go ahead! Let go! Let it pull you, go with it, I encouraged, but the damned thing wouldn't budge. Aided by the steady drumbeat, energy continued to pour into my body. A radiant heat was building at the center of my groin and threatened to scorch my innards. It was too much. I had to stop even though it felt like the beginning of a breakthrough. I was stymied, but not dismayed.

I reasoned that whittling down the intensity of energy penetration to a tolerable level might allow for an eventual collapse of structured-me through the slow-but-sure approach. I experimented with repeating various phrases while continuing the drumbeat and finally settled on, My life is in your hands. The syllables fell into perfect cadence with the drum's rhythm:

My life
My life
My life is in your hands

When I practiced drumming and chanting the phrase, an unusual merging of mind and feeling took place, drawing me downward to a beginning of something. As I trusted its vertical pull, it took me to the fundamental elements of life.

I became one with water—a glacier; the tides and waves; the rain, quenching thirst, nourishing life. I was the sun—a molten fireball, warming the solar system; the light of day; the moon's glow. I was air—the breath of life, sustaining flight; the wind off the ocean. And then I was earth—minerals, rocks, sand; the soil for flora; miniscule in an infinite universe.

Losing myself in the nuclei of these elements was

bringing me to the essence of being, but there had to be more. I knew it would be unproductive to try to think of the something that escaped me, but I tried anyway. I had no recourse—I thought. When I stopped trying, the thinking stopped too. It was suddenly crystal clear: I was afraid to risk sacrificing structured-me to a state of nothingness.

More practice, and then I noticed, after an extended round of drumming, a profound silence pervade the room. The contrast between the vigorous beat and the quiet that immediately followed produced an eerie emptiness. I was drawn to that silence. I again brought the drumming to a maximum tempo and volume, stopped, and waited. The longer I waited, the deeper and more pervasive the silence became. It reached the nadir of purity and I plunged into its amorphous field. An icy chill ricochetted through me; I suspected death was hovering in the background. I lost all sense of dimension. Then I heard a vague sound which very slowly became more audible, becoming separate sounds and then forming into words:

ee, ell, ey, ee
pee, bell, bey, bee
pre-belly baby!

I was at the origin of life, a fetus spinning in a whirlpool. The motion caused a peeling away of the layers of my form, revealing a seed. The action slowed and time came to a halt at ground-zero. I was drifting, suspended. There was no thought, only a sense of pure formlessness. A pulsing, like a heartbeat, floated nearby. Although noise and movement surrounded the flow-space, I remained free of its influence and profoundly at ease.

Without warning, I began tumbling in a vastness, with no up or down. Then I exploded, my atoms flying in all directions. In a flash, I was in pure stillness again, except for tracings of light as if from falling stars.

As I opened my eyes, my attention shifted. Stunned, I realized that the spasm was still intact. To have dissolved that fully into the formless field without resolving the belly constriction was difficult to reconcile. I had little sense of what to do at this point, but I knew that I must again find union with that special kind of force which had originally helped me expel the spasm. I finally gave up trying to figure out what to do and simply waited.

For weeks nothing happened. Then one rainy afternoon the waiting came to an abrupt end—or, rather, a new beginning.

I had settled back in my favorite chair after an intense drumming session. As I opened my eyes I saw, seated in the chair opposite me, a female figure—a kind of universal mother, enveloped in a pulsating aura. She gestured for me to approach, and as I did she grew larger and I became the cosmic pre-belly baby. Soon I was at her bosom, suckling from her warm breast, filled with the serenity I had known only in the pure stillness of my earlier experience. Unexpectedly, I was back in my chair again.

The universal mother was suddenly displaced by an image of an all-powerful universal father. We embraced with deep affection. Again the impression changed as the two figures merged and became one. The universal parent beckoned for me to enter an opening in the lower part of its abdomen, and as I did, an enormous magnetic force sucked the spasm from my gut. My surrender to that transpersonal figure produced within me a limitless sense of freedom. Fresh energies poured through me, leading to a softening of breath, feeding my being with an exquisite calm, and moving gently within me.

My body released a tremendous sigh as I realized the spasm was completely gone. After two years of pain and struggle, I had made my first crossing to transpersonal consciousness.

I took time to assimilate the experiences which had taken me far beyond anything I had previously known. Apparently the Master had burst the seams of my secular consciousness, leaving me exposed to a vast source of raw life-force. The spasm took on a certain rationale too, for it had kept me engaged in making a crossing from a structured-self to pure flow, to an awakening world of wonder and awe. For the next few months I drummed the essence of that flow and studied my notes. The drums made what I sought accessible, and I took every advantage of their midwifery. I was obviously caught up in a longing for euphoria, finding my need of the free spirit irresistible.

Words! Words! At this point I was deeply concerned about the problem of terminology. I preferred not to become involved with semantics, but how was I to describe to others all that had happened?

After a great deal of thought I arrived at the following definitions. For my structured-self I decided on the term *vehicle*. This encompasses: sense impressions tied to the body, keeping one's attention focussed on various manifestations of the five senses; emotions born out of personal desire which sustain a running duality of reactions involving contentment/discontentment, security/insecurity, and so on; and mental activity arising from ego, processing the small personal-self in relation to internal and external phenomena. For the pure spirit realm, I decided on the term *essence*. This encompasses: the noumenal or transpersonal, beyond the above three media; a current or stream of pure feeling flow, a part of the universal vital force, outside time and space, where an omniscient and omnipresent logos operates, where purity translates itself into divine love and spirituality.

The spirit was invariably willing to fill me with a broad spectrum of pleasure, giving me everything, denying me nothing. It was a perfect parent—but demanding as well. My continued initiation included the steady forfeiture of my vehicular-self, and I found this an affront to my personal pride and independence. To submit to some mystical power went against the grain of my lifestyle. Structured-me grew more helpless each time I tapped the essence. Any attempt to defy the free spirit, any assertion of self-rule, evoked harsh reprimands leveled at my nervous system. Sharp twinges of pain would erupt, a clear-cut censure for any separatist indulgences. Still, each time I reentered pure essence, I was rewarded with another round of spirit nourishment.

The spirit was not only dismantling the images of my supposed uniqueness, but fashioning a new reality as well. The life I had lived was unquestionably being uprooted along with a storehouse of beliefs. I became intensely preoccupied with the meaning that my life should have for me. For, if I let go of the vehicle completely, who would I be—what would I be? Sorting out those me's and my's was now indispensable.

It might have been easier if my religious upbringing had been truly spiritual. But as is true for many people, my early conditioning was merely hollow ceremony: a dry ritualistic pablum rather than the nectar of spirit awareness. But now, saturated by the spirit of the Master, I realized new awakenings of essence values. Spirit consciousness meant just naturally feeling love. It was a flow of love pure unto itself, demonstrating its concern for my being, replenishing my body and mind, infusing me with patience and a more tender disposition.

What I had to cultivate was a greater trust of that primary force. But opening myself up to it released tremendous power. Despite my misgivings I was being converted into a conduit for the expression of that power, which now moved like a river through the trunk of my body. The direction the power force took was critical. If the energy flowed downward, it nourished the roots of my nervous system, instilling me with surging vitality. If it zoomed upward, collecting in the cerebral zone, vehicular-me was waiting to seize the life-force for its private purposes.

I found myself laughing. I was losing my ability to think in the usual ways. Yet it was all right; there was nothing to think about in the spirit space. *It* was all. There was also nothing to fear, or to prove; no deadlines or quotas. So there was no room for success or failure. As I became freer of these secular preoccupations, vehicular-me grew suspicious of that kind of relative or personal freedom which has no form. To be one with essence was to be in pure freedom, which meant cutting loose from vehicular-me, continually at loggerheads with all the other persons seeking relative freedom through individual efforts. What lay ahead was the promise that in serving the universal will, I would be drawn closer to the Creator, the source of all that was and is.

But there was also a playful renaissance, leading to lighthearted jubilance which was quite out of character with my previous, studied approach to life. Apparently my sobriety had squelched a joyful, fun-loving spirit long enough. As my restlessness increased, I needed to let go completely, to break out, to remove myself from the familiar. Besides, I was tired of the misery and suffering my patients brought each day, and felt I could get along just fine without being involved with other people's woes. There was no problem; I would drop out.

You can't walk out on the people you are helping, essence said clearly.

Helping! Who's helping? I'm not indispensable; they can find help somewhere else!

As I heard myself responding, I recognized that I had blurted out a truth. As a person I was dispensable, but perhaps the awakening transpersonal-me could be valuable for others. A chill ran through me at the thought there could be a spirit orientation in my work. Stripped of pretenses, I had to admit I was bored when I sat with patients. I had lost the feel of therapy and de-bated whether it had a real purpose any longer—an uncertainty I had never experienced. It was difficult to face the fact that after so many years in a satisfying career I was now just treading water.

Settling for that was not in me, so I began to take inventory, making a list of all the reasons why I should feel reassured about my career. I had the accreditation patients expected of a professional, and was well-informed regarding the course therapy could and should take; I knew how to tap the subconscious and the unconscious; I was skilled in helping patients experience their inner emotions, conflicts and complexes —the repressions that interfered with their finding inner harmony. I was also a fairly realized human being, a concerned, sympathetic and fully dedicated person. Until now. If I could have faulted myself it would have been for trying too hard and taking my responsibilities too seriously with regard to the progress patients made.

All of this had felt so right; it constituted the basis for being able to work in depth—helping others to gain the means to know love, to find happiness, to make something of their lives. I had helped many people in this way. Why had it all turned cold? I reviewed my case load and examined the relationship I had with each patient. I had been helping each in his or her own way, and they were making progress and gaining understanding of themselves and others.

But it was pointless to continue with this shoring up of self. No list could overcome the abysmal flatness which had overtaken me.

My spirit consciousness reasserted itself, not by denigrating past efforts, but simply by showing me that my work had lacked essence. I could catch the outline of a new reality, one which no longer drew solely on the resources of two separate individuals—therapist and patient—but had the spirit available as the source of help. My free spirit was tugging at me to accept this dictum, but my vehicular consciousness continued to hold back.

This spilling back and forth brought me to another truth: I had never tried engaging anyone on the formless spirit plane. Yet, to present vague inferences to patients appeared presumptuous. I could try to reassure them that everything would fall into place, that problems would have a way of taking care of themselves once they became connected to the spirit plane; but even if they believed me, it would be my vehicle giving information to their vehicle, rather than their living that reality first-hand. I could not promise them they would reach the spirit space or, once there, benefit from the experience. Introducing patients to the spirit seemed fraught with pitfalls. Yet I was no longer capable of relating to them in my customary way.

I was deluged with impressions of the past in trying to formulate a future course; but something of the present remained as well, quietly fermenting within me, pushing out old conceptions. The dilemma lessened as I acknowledged I had only to reveal to patients the true person I was becoming—not an authority, not an expert, merely someone in a position of service, allowing the spirit to determine the flow between two people. Proceeding full-steam would leave me completely on my own. *And if you get stuck, who'll bail you out?* vehicular-me kept cautioning. But spirit-me was in process. The issue was what the patients wanted. If they yearned to find their pure, natural, original spirit beings, beyond vehicular consciousness, that would be reason enough to help them do so.

Nevertheless, I couldn't afford to adopt a simplistic

view. All I had to rely on with patients was what I sensed worked for me. The complexities were much greater with them—my whole rationale for being a professional, their turning to me in deep trouble, the responsibility. But the responsibility was an anathema only if I thought of myself as fulfilling a role. To give up the role meant the whole process no longer fitted the reality with which I had associated myself during years of professional training.

The spirit force invaded my consciousness during consultations, continually distracting me with ideas of spirit alternatives. There was no point in resisting. I was being force-fed this new information.

By now I was capable of crossing over into spirit consciousness without relying on the drum. I practiced working backwards from the spirit plane to ordinary consciousness, then forward again. At first I engaged in imaginary activities, such as mowing the lawn or taking a shower, while remaining in the spirit. Eventually I could remain there while actually going about my daily activities. This was a hint that patients could be introduced to the transpersonal plane in a direct manner.

My concern was how to lead patients into that realm, to help them let go of their vehicles, their body consciousnesses, and their emotions, in order to realize the spirit. I would have to develop a blueprint for helping patients to make that crossing.

Drawing on past experiences, I assembled a list of prerequisites which I felt played a part in effecting a transpersonal launch. Included were body relaxation, scanning of mental and emotional activity, breath awareness, spatial centering, and acceptance of energy flow.

By now coming events held a certain fascination for me, since my position with others would be comparable to the Master's with me. However, I was reluctant to deliver that kind of penetrating power. At this point, I was doing a balancing act between the emerging, formless energy which worked by itself, and the years of indoctrination which were so much a part of my functioning. I was confronted with having to assimilate this transitional reality.

I was as ready as I ever would be. But I mistrusted allowing my vehicular-self to select the first candidate. If I was to function in spirit, decisions of this nature would be made for me. This was the first of many rules with which I would be obliged to live. Remaining centered in spirit awareness for several weeks brought no apparent results, and I began to have second thoughts. Then Lynn called, breaking a two-year silence.

L ynn was a shy and apprehensive young woman
who had sought my help over a period of years
in a hit-and-run fashion. She tended to withdraw
whenever her involvement with me came too close to
sensitive material. I knew she had seen several other
therapists as part of her looking-for-a-savior syndrome.
Soon I received a note:

> I have learned over the years that I have one major
> hangup: I make everyone in this world my author-
> ity. I could never let go in therapy for fear of being
> judged. If I could have admitted being afraid of
> someone else's judgment of me, I could have made
> more progress with you. I think you were clever
> enough to know that. I know I resisted your at-
> tempts to reach this fear with all my defenses. One
> of those times you yelled at me. You said I was
> expecting you to correct my problems—not myself.
> Now I know at last what the hell you were talking
> about.

Basically, Lynn lacked faith in her ability to manage her
own life. Her attempts to find herself in work were
half-hearted, and poor relationships with others com-
pounded her self-deprecatory attitude. Even though
her first marriage had broken up, she was still saving

herself for the right man. This romantic illusion kept her searching busily for an ideal soul-mate.

I empathized with Lynn's unhappiness, and often wished I could do more on her behalf. I was torn between my helplessness and a desire to involve her in experiences that might aid her growth. I clung to the notion that perhaps time and reality would wear away her child-bound image of fragility and release the substantial person I considered her to be.

Lynn had had several lovers since her divorce; but Hal, the most recent, had been special. She had once said, I felt I had more of a relationship with him than with anyone I'd ever known. Hal died suddenly of a heart attack. Depressed and feeling very alone, Lynn began to experience a choking sensation soon after he was buried. It kept her awake at night and periodically triggered episodes of panic.

Treating Lynn's fear of strangulation presented no special difficulty. Professional-me knew that having her yell or scream while she allowed the repressed emotions lodged within her to override the fear or guilt of her vehicular-self probably would have ventilated and unknotted the binding conflict that the symptom represented. I might also have explored with her some of the root experiences that contributed to the throat constriction.

But now I was prepared to introduce her to the spirit process, provided she was willing.

As I explained the process, she was on the edge of her chair, as she often was when she was concerned about listening attentively. She was eager to try it. I did not question her quick acceptance, but I noticed her voice carried an anxious giggle. My spirit was ready to proceed despite this indication of her apparent insecurity. It was her clinging to vehicular safety that I wanted to help translate into spirit involvement—if that was possible.

Although spirit-me was ready to go full steam ahead, professional-me was wary, suggesting I still had little experience in taking this major step. Weeks before I had experimented with acquaintances, using a preinduction phase to spirit experiencing. It was a method that seemed to give some indication of a person's inclination and ability to separate himself from his persona. I had learned that the more attached the person was to others, to career, to material possessions, the less free he was to let go of his vehicular-self.

Since this preinduction test had already demonstrated its value, I used it with Lynn. She was able to make the necessary vehicular separation. We talked about this afterwards and considered how she might apply what had happened to her choking symptom.

She was excited when I saw her the following week. Her eyes danced elatedly as she spoke:

> Whenever I would think of Hal's death, I would say to myself, The vehicle is telling me it wants to die. I had to say this a number of times before it registered. I had to choose different words to say the same thing—that the vehicle was trying to kill

me, that the vehicle was feeling that it couldn't live or didn't want to live without him. Even at night, I used the same words, and now the feeling of strangulation is almost gone.

I questioned Lynn a bit more.

I'd get a feeling that I would want to run out of the room and tear my clothes off. Then I would draw back from my vehicle somewhat. I can't really describe it. I just know I was able to do it, and now I realize I was separating myself from various parts of me. I can get further away for longer periods of time now. Along with the feeling of strangulation, I would get a terrible sinking feeling in the pit of my stomach. I'm surprised now that it isn't there.

I reserved judgment concerning Lynn's use of her spirit-self to split herself off from the vehicle's control. There was still the matter of her going beyond preliminaries and entering the spirit space. When I suggested going further she said, Let's do it.
That was enough for me. Lynn consented to let me tape the proceedings.

I feel I am romping in space, swinging, jumping and running. I want to go higher. A moment ago I could feel the vehicle was holding me. When I said, It's holding me, I went higher, like I was in an elevator, going very fast, very high, where the sky was a dark blue, almost black, very close to the stars. Now I see somebody, another me, on a perch, like a bird. There is a chain, a very long, thin, shiny, gold chain attached from the me on the perch to the me floating around in space. I said, It's holding me, and the chain dropped away. Then I floated up again. You are floating up there, too. But you are on a platform. I'm out in the space. It's quite dark now. That's because I'm far away from what I was attached to. You're still way out there, still on your platform. I'm just drifting. We are both drifting around. That's all I want to do. I don't want to go back down.

I feel we have traveled as far as we can. The earth is a pinpoint. I see it through the clouds, just a pinpoint. Now we are drifting around within a huge ball that surrounds the earth—just drifting inside it. The earth and the space are encased inside this ball. There are very bright and sparkly stars. The inside of the ball has a crust to it like stucco. It's all glistening. The color is navy blue, very dark, light and misty. It's sort of frosty. We are just drifting around the inside of the ball.

You are still on your platform, just the way you are ordinarily. But I'm barefooted and in something very soft and white. It's cold out there but I don't feel the cold. I feel light and very free.

There's no sound in my space. When I clap my hands there's no sound, and I like it. I don't have a feeling that I've lost my hearing. I have the feeling that something in the space takes away the sound. When I'm with you, I don't follow you, you follow me. I don't mind that you are there, but I wouldn't mind if you went away either.

I feel tired and I'm sitting on the raft with you.

You're in a chair. I'm sitting on the edge, just resting.

Although I had said nothing up to this point, I remained fully involved from my spirit plane. Afterwards, Lynn had an urge to recap what happened.

I'm amazed that I have a body. For a moment I forgot that I had one. I'm sort of surprised to see it. When I opened my eyes, I saw my legs and my hands. I felt my body again. It was sort of like waking up and discovering that I had feet, legs, arms, hands and a head—that all these things were there all the time. It's a funny feeling, sort of a surprise, like I didn't have any feeling within myself all the time we were doing this. There was nothing going on in my body to make me conscious of it all the while.
She laughed.
Well, it makes me feel good. I feel happy about the experience. It felt nice. I liked it. I felt as if I escaped from everything.

When you say everything, what do you mean?

Me! I got away from me. I escaped from all my emotions, all that clutter; it really feels like freedom from debris in my head.

Was there any mental activity that was interfering?

No, I didn't have any trouble.

The vehicle didn't intrude?

Just at the very beginning. I had a little trouble switching while listening to you. I think I was a little confused as to how to carry out the instructions. But then it fell into place very quickly and each step went very easily after that.

You talk about escaping from yourself.

I guess that's the way I felt. I felt very happy when I was out there. There were no movies to see, no people around. You were there part of the time, not all of the time, not in the beginning. There was no stimulation of any kind. There was just the space, but I felt happy anyway. I didn't need anything else. I was just there romping and feeling good. There were no conflicts, no problems.

The implication is that when you're out there you're running away from life, from your life.

It must be an escape because out there there's nothing that's required of me. Down on earth is where it's at, where I have to function. Up there I didn't have to do anything.

You mentioned you experienced me in the space with you.

You were more in shadow than I was. I don't know what that means. You were more in the darker atmosphere. I think your presence meant more but I don't know how.

Is there anything else you want to say?

No, except that, if I separate myself, I feel free. I just feel happy with nothing going on and nothing being said to me. I'm not doing anything. I just feel happy when I'm able to separate myself from the vehicle. That's what I discovered this past week. I felt better about the separation. But sometimes I feel certain ways, and I don't know how to talk to those feelings. Then I get kind of panicky.

When you say you get panicky, aren't you saying that sometimes the vehicle takes over and sends out messages that you experience as panic?

That's what happens. I guess I'm trying to get an image of what the spirit is, because I don't have an image of it.

The intellect of the vehicle cannot understand the spirit space. It will keep trying to get into the act, to nullify it, to hack away, to undermine, or join it by creating images in order to ruin it.

I do experience the vehicle joining in to make trouble for spirit-me. But I didn't know how to handle it. I didn't know why the vehicle was there. I thought I wasn't able to separate myself well enough when the vehicle kept reappearing.

It will take time and patience to comprehend what's going on between your vehicle and spirit spaces.

My vehicle lets me have little portions. It let me do that just now. I don't know whether it thinks, I'll let her have a little bit and maybe she'll be quiet for awhile.

The fact that you can see what's going on is important.

I notice that the spirit is not very strong yet. Sometimes the vehicle takes over and jumps on it. When it does, I just have to let it go because I can't work with it. It just chokes me. Then I try to deal with it another time.

Is there anything else?

I experienced a sense of elation in that space.

If you had a girdle on for a week straight and then took it off, you would probably have the same sense of elation.

I never anticipated that Lynn would be as self-sufficient as she was in the spirit environment. I felt rather sheepish that this ability was within her all the time, while I had used standard methods of therapy—which generally drew blanks—to help in her personal growth. If she didn't need me or anyone else that much while in spirit space, then her capacity for self-maintenance was simply obfuscated by a vehicle which kept her bound to illusionary images.

Identifying the real Lynn became a bit fuzzy too. Was she the person preoccupied with coping, dealing with her deep-seated insecurities? Or was she Lynn the spirit? Lynn could only conceptualize herself as real when she was her vehicular self, completely immersed in everyday affairs. Only when she was *doing something* was she not running away from life. Within that context the spirit space had to be unreal, since it was a place where nothing was required of her. Surrender to the natural flow of the spirit was taboo—even though it produced a yielding to bliss of and by itself, even though it offered contentment without dependence on secular stimulation from people or things. I realized from her pattern that even though she had been touched in this way she wouldn't be back for awhile.

I cherished having experienced even briefly the open, natural, carefree spirit-Lynn. But if her structured-self renounced the spirit for the sake of a preformed secular reality, her spirit's doom was predictable. There-fore, when Lynn described her crossing to the trans-personal as an escape, I felt that she had put her finger on the pulse of every generation's search and struggle in terms of spirit and vehicular identification.

But the issue of escapism that Lynn presented also raised other considerations. Perhaps Lynn was con-veying a deep uneasiness of having her life-style af-fected by the spirit. She still lived among other people, with all the expectations that society extolled as worth-while. She would now be confronted, as I was, with reconciling the spirit with all of that. When I considered her predicament, I could understand her rush to return to the familiar patterns of her structured life. It was ob-vious, too, that to maintain and enhance a spirit aware-ness in the midst of people who were often antagonistic to the very essence of spirit would challenge other patients as well.

I expected that in time Lynn would again contact me, but now I was prepared to move on to other spirit-patient encounters. To test the value of the spirit process, I would need to engage someone who was more committed to risk.

Wayne was an ongoing patient with an adventuresome nature. Perhaps I was stacking the deck for a more favorable outcome when I outlined a spirit undertaking to him, but in any case he favored changing the direction of our work, and I felt he was ready for the big leap.

Perseverance is crucial to personal growth, and Wayne had a dogged determination that kept him returning week after week. The direction his therapy took was in keeping with his need to establish himself in a career. Of course, as we worked together, problems in other areas of his life drew our attention, but only briefly.

Wayne's early life had been severely affected by the limitations of a hapless household. Both his parents were handicapped by inadequacies in education and personal development and had been hard-pressed to sustain their marginal existence. Wayne had floundered in this setting. His father had been unable to guide him properly; and although his mother's warmth and affection were reassuring, her lack of worldliness had added to his misgivings of having no one to turn to for understanding or help. This had resulted in a tendency to overcompensate.

No one pushed me around. I had a reputation for using my fists on any kid that came near me. I heard repeated warnings from my father to be rough and tough, or I'd wind up as a pansy. Not only that, but when I went out to play in the neighborhood we lived in, there was usually some other kid waiting to beat me up.

Wayne's athletic abilities offered a partial outlet for his pugnacity. Being selected for an all-state high school basketball team had provided him with a degree of personal recognition. However, he had little interest in academic studies. Poor relationships with teachers, along with eventual ineligibility in sports, had forced him to drop out of high school without receiving a diploma.

Once I was bounced from the team, I had to study if I was to finish school. So I bowed out. Sports was a way of being on top, of feeling important. But then, I had to come down to earth. When I did, I felt very inadequate. I really thought of myself as being too stupid to learn. I put up a front and told myself, Graduating is a big nothing; I don't need that piece of paper to get along.

With a natural flair for mechanics, Wayne had turned to race car driving. During one of his sessions with me, he had been able to see through his desire for fame and fortune.

It was another grand illusion. It became easy for me to think big. I finished second out of twenty-five entrants the first race I entered. Everybody cheered me. From then on, I was on cloud nine.

Gradually Wayne had given up his daredevil penchant and turned to a career in flying. He applied himself with increasing seriousness, passing one technical rating after another. He was now managing a charter flight company which he had organized.

Wayne was in a jovial mood when he arrived for the first spirit session. I considered it necessary that Wayne first establish himself securely in spirit awareness so he could use that plane of consciousness for clearing away vehicular problems. He remained fully immersed in spirit space for over twenty minutes, during which he scarcely spoke. I had placed myself in spirit consciousness also, but his revelations afterwards best describe what occurred.

I felt calm when we started. After following your instructions, I seem to have been transported to another space. I could look straight down from a beautiful snow-capped mountaintop with glacial cliffs on each side to a fantastic lake below. I felt a flood of energy rise up from within me. It got as high as my shoulders and then slowly subsided as I relaxed. A person was standing on the edge of a high diving board. There was an enormous amount of activity going on below where people were scurrying about. The figure on the board made a long, suspended dive in slow motion which ended in a triple somersault. There was a feeling of complete freedom in being able to perform any maneuver. Then I was projected outwards. I had an unreal and shaky feeling about what was happening. Something within me kept trying to pull me back. But I kept going out anyway, further than I had ever been. On two or three occasions the inner force tried to get me to jump up from my chair, to stop what we were doing. It was commanding me, Don't go any further; call it off. I let myself feel it and kept going. Then I sat up in my chair in order to sense more of your plane of consciousness.

A huge wall appeared in outer space, as if in a dream. I didn't resist it. I merely experienced it, and it gradually melted away. But it didn't melt from the top as a wall of ice would normally do. This melted from the bottom. A fraction of the wall remained standing for a brief time, but eventually that disappeared, too. Once the wall dissolved, I was propelled into a vaster space. I tried to sense what it was I was feeling. At one point there were two objects that met. I didn't know whether it was our planes making contact. Then I started to get tired. The mental activity did not close in. It was just that I didn't want to go on any longer. At that point my body started to ache with fatigue.

I asked him to expand on a number of things.

At no time did I feel or think, How will I get back, will I disintegrate? It was difficult enough to handle the problem of moving that far out without worrying about making it back. I can never remember allowing myself that degree of freedom without having any form to depend on for that length of time. I've had fleeting sensations like that at different moments of my life, but it always closed in so fast that I never had a chance to know it like I did today. I feel I should be able to duplicate the experience with additional practice. What happened is a milestone for me and a possible stepping stone for my growing further. I feel very relaxed, but I'm not jumping up and down for joy, either. I don't feel any great, big high. But I must say again that, to me, the key to this whole experience was when I felt the entire wall melt away.

I had a special interest in knowing whether my being in spirit consciousness had been of any value to him.

Your space wasn't of any special security to me when we first started. I didn't say to myself, I have his space so now it's safe for me to project myself out. Instead I went there on my own. But when I came back, I sensed something. I felt very close to another force that had entered my space. There was a feeling of oneness about it. When I sat up in my chair and looked directly ahead, I became aware of a flame out there. I didn't relate it to being you. But it was where you were sitting. Then all of a sudden the wall started to melt from the bottom up.

The following week Wayne supplied me with impressions of what had happened in the interim. Most significant was a developing intensity of vehicular and spirit activity, as if both life-forces were vying to assert their strength as Wayne watched from the sidelines.

I flew one of the seaplanes we have based at the airport last week. After landing on the river, I strolled along the bank near the water. Then I stretched out and listened to the wind. It was a cloudless day with the flowers in full bloom. I stayed there for an hour. My mind was clear, and I drifted right out into space. I felt suspended in that vast area of blue like I did with you last time. I'm not sure, but I believe that person, me, lying on the bank of that river is more of the way I really am—that peaceful person with no boundaries and no frames. I realized, too, that I'd been searching all of my life for some preconceived person I thought I had to be, but which really isn't me at all. I sensed that I could be more of a total person if I gave in to more of my spirit. Up to this point I've said to myself, Yes, this psychology stuff is great; but if you go too far, how do you know you'll be able to control what happens? Since I've been involved in spirit space that attitude seems to have gone by the boards.

I also noticed this week how the vehicle's mental activity kept harassing me. I remember driving the car to work and my brain stirring up thoughts about decisions I would need to make later in the day. It kept me continually on edge, putting me in the position that if I didn't solve the problems right then and there, some terrible misfortune would occur. I found that I could stop the mental static just by saying, This thing is trying to zing me again. Every time it would start up I would say to myself, It's trying to grab me; it's after me again. It would immediately stop but only for a short while. It took that kind of constant effort to relax and be able to look out the window and enjoy the scenery. After two to three hours of observing that mental pressure, my stomach began to tighten up and a sharp pain developed in my shoulder. In a way I felt more discomfort this past week as a result of seeing what was going on. It seemed that the cure might be worse than the sickness.

When I saw Wayne the following week, he was as preoccupied as before with the contending vehicular and spirit forces.

Spirit space took over several times this week while my eyes were wide open. It just popped in for no apparent reason. It usually happened while I was busy in some activity. It would project me out into space. Then I'd come back to where I was before the space shot occurred. It had the effect of stopping my overworked mental activity—stopping it cold. It's hard to put a label on it, but it had a quieting effect, like it was slowing me down to half my activity rate. I'm really getting bored with that busy-ness in my head. The fact is that I'm also getting bored with some of the people around me. Yesterday for example, I was talking to some of the help at work. They wanted to ramble on without having anything worthwhile to say. I had this overpowering urge to get the hell away, out into the fresh air. It left me feeling very fidgety and agitated.

In addition, I found out something the last couple of nights that I didn't want to admit to myself. Evidently, I am quite insecure when I am by myself. I noticed this *alone* feeling the other night while my wife, Karen, was away visiting her folks for the week. I could never talk about it before. I think I knew it was there, but I always rationalized the problem away. I'm also sensing that the reason I got married was based, partly at least, on my nervousness about being alone. This fear is deeply rooted within me, even when I fly. I really saw it surface last night while I was in the house by myself. My vehicle was trying to get me to go here, there, anywhere, to get me away from that emotion. In the past I would ask myself what was causing me to be this way. But now, going back into my history, putting it on to something back there, doesn't interest me. Instead I said to myself, Here I am; it's not me but the vehicle that is acting up. Somehow I'm less annoyed at myself for feeling that.

Being able to experience myself outside the vehicle gives me a chance to see how it is able to pull me back under its control. When the vehicle is stripped down, I know it's going to reveal that I haven't grown and developed enough to handle the pressures it imposes on me. Maybe I haven't been in spirit space long enough to know how to use it better in everyday living. The vehicle has been able to control the spirit within me because, without the vehicle, I would have been unable to manage at all.

Maybe if I had more access to spirit, my reliance on the vehicle wouldn't be that necessary. I do know that the two have to become compatible eventually.

It was very clear to me how he had previously been stuck trying to use his vehicle to reshape his vehicle. Now he had the ability to leave the vehicle and observe its activity from the transpersonal realm. This was a step he had never been able to take while our work had remained limited to the person-to-person field.

At first, when I went into my space, even before you mentioned yours, I had the awareness of another space—something very close, a good feeling. What touched me is that we could be in this vastness, feel comfortable in enjoying it, without any type of strain. There was no hardship, no commitment, nothing I had to give. It was such an easy flow; it surprised me. I didn't have to perform. When we began, I felt my space was on a lower plane. I thought I had to come up to your plane. At first, I couldn't do that. Then my space came up to your wavelength by itself. After that, I stopped comparing mine with yours.

Despite our progress in spirit communion, Wayne could not expect to relate to people in daily activity on an exclusively spirit-to-spirit plane. He was confronted with reconciling his spirit consciousness with the full range of vehicular forms around him. It occurred to me that since Wayne's spirit was beginning to see his vehicle more clearly from a separate vantage point, it might be valuable for his spirit consciousness to see into

—and perhaps through—the vehicular boundaries of others. So I presented Wayne with new instructions. I asked him to slip out of his vehicular form and release his spirit consciousness. He was then to enter my form with his spirit. Once within my form, he was to live out all awareness of the interior of my person, and then return to the expansiveness of his spirit space.

What's happened to your vehicle, Wayne?

It doesn't exist.

What about my vehicle?

I'm having a strong sensation. There seems to be a depth and a shining light way down. It feels like it's surrounding me, and I'm inside it.

What about your spirit?

It's very hard to feel it now.

I suggested to Wayne that he leave my form and establish his spirit presence more fully before attempting to reenter my vehicle.

I'm having trouble pulling out of your space. I have a feeling that your space is overwhelming.

Can you describe this more?

It's a sensation, like something I'm finding too much to handle.

Who is it that can't handle it?

As I'm sitting here now, it feels like it's flooding me, more like an enormous tank of water. The water is coming over the top, and yet it doesn't seem to bother me. It's a feeling of things being out of control, but I still feel a calmness down deep.

Let it unfold as much as it can.

It's almost like sinking into water or quicksand. It's a calm sensation, but there seems to be an enormous area of—now the flooding is easing. The overwhelming sensation is disappearing.

Just let it out.

I'm still in your space. At first, it was kind of uncontrollable. I can feel my own spirit space deep down now and a vast area of calmness.

Wayne's experience, although brief, had been intense. It was time to stop. I suggested that we continue with this approach at our next meeting, but it turned out to be a mistake.

Wayne was quite upset when I saw him the following week.

I seem to have had a lot of trouble trying to relate to what we talked about last week, the idea of getting into other people's vehicles. That gave me more static than anything we've done so far. I don't relate well to that. Spirit space is something else again. I feel great in that flow. But it's virtually impossible for me to be in the spirit plane and deal with society. The way I figure it, either I become a hermit on a mountaintop, or I give up the idea of the spirit. When I'm in spirit space, I don't have any boundaries. I like that type of feeling. It's becoming clearer to me about these two frequencies I'm on. Either I'm operating with the vehicle on an achieving kick, or else I'm feeling open in spirit space and not being sucked into the vehicle's demands. But I don't function well within someone else's vehicle. Maybe I just don't give a damn about working that part of it out with other people. I asked myself during the week whether I really care that much about other people to bother.

He revealed that he had tried a cram course at home in order to be prepared for another attempt at vehicular entry. I sensed a desire on his part not to disappoint me. I skirted this and gave him whatever reassurance I could before again asking him to enter my vehicular space.

I'm experiencing your form. It's an enormous flying balloon. There's a tremendous volume of air or gas that's rushing into it and filling it up. My vehicle and my spirit are going along with the intake of the balloon as it's being inflated. There's a great flooding feeling of gas expanding within me to the point of bursting or blowing up—as if this force is inflating me along with the balloon.

I recalled my body spasm. For a moment I braced my-self for a comparable buildup within Wayne's body as a result of the rapid accumulation of energy. But this was going to be different.

Now there's an escape of air coming out of the port-holes of the balloon and the stress is easing. The forms of our vehicles have disappeared, and our two spirits are linked up, tumbling in space, like spacecrafts linked together. There is a light glow of gold, a warm feeling that's flowing in, an enormous universal glow has taken over.

See if this glowing energy can fill your spirit space and supply you its power.

I feel it's transferred to part of me now.

Let it expand to the fullest. Let it express itself in what-ever ways it wants to. Also, breathe the spirit so it can be absorbed by your nervous system.

There's a fantastic amount of power building up, like the Northern Lights flowing back and forth with a surplus amount of energy.

You felt it was too much for you to handle; it was getting the better of you. But once you allocated the power, letting it shift to spirit space, there was no problem.

Yes, that's true. I can see that. I realize I'll feel more secure in going into another person's vehicle if I'm in spirit. I know there are no boundaries that can hurt me when I'm into spirit space. I don't have to protect myself then. I can see how I can work things out better now on a spirit level. I couldn't understand that before in being just the vehicle. It's clear to me suddenly how the vehicle hassles, how it's intent on protecting its boundaries, its form, its secular ideas, the preservation of itself above everything else.

Since the movement of spirit and vehicular involvement was transpiring so well, I asked Wayne to move beyond my vehicle and take himself into an alternate form.

I want you to let any vehicular form come into view, a vision of a vehicle you would allow into your space. It can be animal or human. It can materialize from anything. When you're ready, you can enter that vehicle, repeating what you did with me.

It's a woman. My vehicle has a lot of trouble with this particular person. Now I'm free of my vehicle, and I'm zeroing in on her with my spirit, into her form. There's an overload of negative feeling within her. She's the daughter of the majority stockholder of the company. I've had no other choice but to keep her on the payroll. I'm trying to feel if there's any spirit within her. I can't feel any there. All I can experience is her jamming mental noise. Now I've left her space. I couldn't see any point in staying there any longer. Everything got jumbled up. I had to get away. I continued right on out of her vehicle. I could feel myself relax as I left and felt a sense of calmness when I got outside her. Now I'm out in spirit space again with no boundaries.

One way for Wayne to work through whatever stress he was feeling was for him to repeat the venture. This would afford him a means to gain additional clarity, like seeing a movie for the second time and noticing details overlooked during the first viewing.

This time I felt I wanted to stay around a little longer. I wanted to experience her vehicle a little more, and I did. A couple of things are clearer in regard to what makes this person tick and operate as she does. I'm out of her vehicle and back in spirit space again. I feel a lot more energy and power within me now.

I want you to try the same thing once more, with the increased understanding you've gained from being in her vehicle, plus the added power you now feel from your spirit flow.

I can see how this person is fouled up. It's so clear. This woman has given up on any spirit life. She's probably one of the most unhappy people I've met. It's so clear how she's made everyone around her unhappy. I can almost tell you why—to the T. Funny, I feel sorry for her in one sense, and then in another way I don't at all. This woman has completely given up on her spirit and is just waiting for death.

How do you mean?

It's like it's a fact. It's like I know, like I just know it's absolutely true. It's amazing. It's like this vast knowledge is inside me. It's that I know and there's nothing more to say about it.

The knowing seems to be related to spirit knowing, I gather.

Yes! If I went into an experience like that with just my vehicle, it would be deadly with this person. Right now, there's no conflict at all. There's nothing that bothers me as a result of my spirit knowing and being aware of this truth.

Now I know what knowing means. There's no problem about its being this or that. It's absolute. It's perfectly clear, as simple as that. It's so obvious that unless they pack her up and move her off the grounds there'll only be trouble and turmoil. The amazing thing is this *absolute* feeling. It has nothing to do with a decision. It just is that way. It's an absolute knowing, and the spirit going along with the vehicle is the key. I was trying to do this at home during the week with just my vehicle. That isn't going to work, is it?

His question didn't need an answer. Furthermore, my thoughts were on something else—the nature of his euphoria. I had often noticed Wayne's use of the superlative when describing what he deemed to be spirit success. In this formative stage, he was bound to be impressed by an identity larger than his vehicular consciousness. It was understandable, in being tossed back and forth between vehicular and spirit consciousness, that Wayne would be attempting to adjust his conceptions of himself. His excitement at being able to know that woman from a holistic, spirit perspective was interpreted by his vehicle as extraordinary. Actually, there was nothing exceptional about such absolute knowing when viewed from the consciousness of spirit. Spirit awareness is not a personal attribute, even though it might be felt as unique at the time of its experiencing.

I needed a breather to digest all the things that had happened. Dipping into the spirit flow with Lynn and Wayne had heightened my curiosity concerning the nature of that communication. There was no way for me to describe these spirit dyads, yet I felt compelled to explore the process. It had a serene quality, but was outside the realm of sleep or ordinary daydreaming. Slipping into the transpersonal plane reminded me of walking out of a stuffy, overheated room into the clear, brisk night air.

The words we had used to describe our realizations of the spirit were abstractions—expressing, through metaphor, points of contact where form and formlessness joined at the wellspring of creation.

The purest experiencing for me manifested during interludes of silence, a kind of trans-time/space continuum, during which we were fully immersed in the total surround of spirit. At such moments, I vibrated not only on that plane but in complete harmony with another human being tuned to that same all-embracing force. The communicative flow during such episodes was more profound than I had ever known. There were unspoken depths of understanding resulting from being integrally one with that purity, beyond personal identity, uniqueness, or individuality. I was left with one persistent intuition: if spirit dyad was beyond words, then it was preliterate, preverbal, universal, known to us at birth—an endowed consciousness.

I was now ready to go on, but Wayne was stuck with an internal tug-of-war.

> I feel like the vehicle and the spirit forces are in a death struggle with each other. The vehicle has run me most of my life and now it's losing out. The pushing back and forth is hard to take. There are instances now where the spirit has its own ideas. Before I did things completely on the basis of the vehicle's thinking. I don't like the idea of being split this way. I want to get the vehicle and the spirit working together so that they function harmoniously. Numerous times this past week, I have caught myself whipping the vehicle. I don't want to do that, just as I don't want the vehicle putting the spirit down. I need to have them compatible while I retain the flow of spirit.

I was waiting for spirit to manifest a guideline for me. I'd noticed how difficult it was for me to just sit idly by while waiting to receive some clue regarding a next step. This tension existed within me, despite all my resolution to trust spirit wisdom. All I could do was wait.

We had Karen's friends over for the Labor Day weekend. The couple she invited couldn't make up their minds until the last minute whether they were coming or not. We go through this game with them all the time. Finally they decided they would stay the weekend. Mack, the husband, is on a full-blown ego trip. My sister and brother-in-law, Bruce, showed up later in the day. I was getting sick of their drinking and carrying on. But I tried to keep busy so as not to let those things bother me. Late that afternoon, I took my nephew for a ride in the seaplane. When I returned they were still at it. I can't stand being around my sister and brother-in-law for more than an hour or so anyway. They argue and fight constantly—going around in circles. I was listening to Mack and Bruce snowing each other. I've been listening more to people recently than I did in the past. Mack was explaining something about his job, trying to impress the others. It would have been comical if it wasn't so pathetic. The stereo was blasting away while they kept boozing it up. I don't like to drink or to be associated with drinking anymore.

Finally, by nine that evening I had had it up to my ears. I said to myself, Why am I going through all this nonsense? Then Mack said something trivial, and I blew my stack. I said I wished everyone would pack up and go home. It was like I put a pillow full of chicken feathers to the fan. But I couldn't control myself. Everyone just stopped dead in their tracks. I never chased anybody out of my house before. Some time ago, in a fit of anger like that, I would have probably broken someone's head. This time I went off into the woods with our cats trailing behind me. I didn't return until everyone had left. I had a terrible feeling inside me that was saying, Man! You can't function like that! But then I had a sudden changeover—a solid feeling within me which countered, Bullshit! You don't have to put up with that.

Before, I always had a guilty feeling if I did such a thing. But this time I didn't feel at all guilty. I don't even feel guilty now while I'm telling you this. If those two bastards weren't drinking so much, weren't stewed to the gills, weren't so insensitive, they would have known that the whole affair had gone far enough.

After it was over, Karen complained that I did it because I had no feeling for her friends. I told her about another couple we know, Randy and his wife. They visited us a few weeks ago and left early because I needed to get to bed. Randy's done that with me. We have a relationship, and I don't have to be concerned with niceties. When I pointed that out to Karen, she shut up.

I want you to repeat what you've done before. Only this time you're to enter that social scene with just your spirit consciousness, stripped of your vehicle. Let your vehicle dissolve. Sense from your spirit plane whatever comes to you while you're immersed in that situation.

I can see that my vehicle is overreacting in the scene. It's become tense even though my spirit is there. I can see the possibility of having a different reaction in the situation. Now I'm seeing the vehicle on one side of the room and the spirit on the other. I'm observing the goings on from a third point, seeing the whole scene. There's a lot of muttering, with people's faces mouthing things. My spirit can't flow in all that commotion. All their vehicles are racing at full speed, competing with one another. There's no room for my spirit to function from that third point of reference. There's nothing I can do unless I want to stay there for another four hours and suffer.

It was obvious Wayne was experiencing alienation—but not vehicular alienation concerned with acceptance and approval. He was struggling with a social situation which he had outgrown. He assumed it didn't allow for his spirit, but at this point that was all he conceived he could do. My thoughts were cut short as I noticed Wayne had tears in his eyes.

I know it seems strange that I would be crying. But they're tears of joy. You don't realize what it means to be free from worrying about how these people feel about me. They think I have nothing because of my indifference to those earthly things, such as boozing it up and playing Mr. Big. Actually, I'm beginning to feel that I have everything. It's when I was wrapped up in that clutter that I had nothing. When the vehicle had its way, I was forced to depend on such people for a handout of approval, just like they depended on me for the same kind of nonsense. To be able to live through my spirit, free from that childishness, is a real accomplishment for me. If these people can't accept me as I am, it doesn't matter to me anymore. It's peculiar, but I don't feel obligated to anybody in that old way, not even to you. If I don't want to do this sort of thing with you anymore, I can just tell you and that's that. I don't have to say to myself, the way I did in the past, What does he expect of me; what does he want of me? and then try to please you. There isn't that type of flow between us now. I have a tremendous respect for you as a guide, as a tool, but I don't feel that I owe you anything. I never experienced that before with you. Now I have a good feeling about your person, but I don't need you. Maybe I'm becoming more independent by becoming more dependent on the universe and its flow. That's where I get this strong, healthy feeling of gratification. I realize that this power is always available. I don't have to appeal to other people for it. That power is out there for me to use for my spirit. What's becoming clearer to me too is that I'm not going to be able to function with certain people. In the past, my vehicle wouldn't let me think in those terms. It would get me to try, try, and try again in order not to feel the possibility of failure. I find it easier to be with certain people in business dealings or on a personal level. But there are others I just won't be able to make it with—spirit flow or not. And I don't want to.

The next time I saw Wayne he was eager to relate examples of his freer dealings with other people.

> Maybe that session we had last week hit home. The other day at the airport I gave one of the linemen a real tongue-lashing for failing to carry out certain safety regulations. I was concerned about a possible crash if the landing precautions weren't handled properly. I noticed that I got angry as hell—as fast as I ever did—but I didn't get into an emotional stew over it. Before, I'd get mad not only in my head but inside me as well. This time it didn't affect me personally. It was like my body tension flipped off. I walked away from the whole scene as if it didn't happen.

His progress had to be measured against the larger view, which was to what extent the vehicle still held sway in his functioning. Extending our effort hinged on clearing out more of the vehicle's influence. To do this, I asked him to do a turnabout—to go into his vehicular self. Once inside the form of his person, he was to stay as long as possible, and then he was to leave and return to the fullest measure of spirit experience.

> I had trouble going in and coming out. There was an instantaneous image of my father and a lot of related flashbacks of my life. I experienced a dark cloud surrounding my spirit. There was also a strong, tight, gripping feeling that held the spirit prisoner within me. Finally I felt my spirit force break away and very rapidly propel me into the spirit field outside. That's where I am now, separate from my vehicle. There was a slow acceleration

and a lot of drag before the spirit force could break free and move out.

Wayne's vehicular resistance reminded me of my own struggle and the feelings of dread that arose when I faced the loss of a conceptualized self as form. The vehicle's consciousness could only conceive the existence of something if it was engaged in the process of thinking about it. It didn't matter whether the thing to be thought about was an emotion, an attitude, a desire, or a belief. As long as it could carry on the mental process of thinking about this or that, it could maintain the illusion that thinking about things was life itself. I understood very well that Wayne's vehicle would defend itself against a formless spirit force which in no way operated on thinking-about, but which was the essence of unformed energy. To weaken his vehicle's control, I asked Wayne to again dive into his form, to dwell there, to really look, and then to return to his spirit space with as much awareness as possible.

> It's very much like last time. There was a kind of collision as the spirit tried to go inside. The vehicle was blocking the entrance. When I got further into it, I saw some scenes around death, a dog being run over by a car when I was young. Then my mother's funeral flashed by, along with a picture of seeing a friend of mine rescued from being drowned.

It was clear from my own path that these morbid associations were typically used by the vehicle to abort any further efforts at releasing spirit power. I called on him to make one final invasion of his vehicle.

I'm out again. There were some additional flash-
backs and mirror reflections of past stages of my
life, scenes in which my vehicle had control over
my life. Just when I was ready to leave the vehicle's
space, I had a strong urge to explore deeper. There
was a sensation of falling down a shaft with increasing speed. I had a terrible sick feeling along with
the thought, When you hit bottom, you'll be dead.
The speed kept accelerating as the funnel got narrower. Suddenly the movement broke out horizon-
tally. I didn't hit bottom. There was a great relief
that came from not being destroyed. Once that
happened, the force of the plunge disintegrated
and in a flash broke out into the spirit space. I had
the feeling of not being afraid anymore.

Wayne was unaware of the significance of his last
vehicular entry. The change of direction of the energy
force, from anticipated self-destruction to a bursting
forth into the spirit domain with its accompanying dilu-
tion of fear, was apparently the result of a transition
from a vehicular consciousness to the source of spirit.
The vehicle's preconception was that all would be lost
by a collapse into oblivion and nothingness. Yet all that
happened was, at the point of transfer, Wayne lost his
consciousness of structure. For a moment there was
simply a vacuum, a void. But then, within that empty
space, spirit could make its presence known.
Before Wayne left, he volunteered a statement.

Once you've lived in spirit, you don't forget it.
I've been in that spirit area enough to know that it
really exists. You could have described it to me all

day long, but I wouldn't have really understood. Now I truly know it for what it is, where it is, and what it feels like when I'm into it.

If I asked you to describe your vehicle, you wouldn't have any difficulty doing so. You would tell me your height, weight, hair color, something about your personality, your virtues and foibles, your goals and ideas about life. But what about your spirit? If I ask you to describe that to me, what can you say?

It flows. It's a flowing type of force, like an enormous river. It's a peaceful flow, with few currents, no rapids. It's vast. I really don't know it as form. If I try to put a form to it, I have trouble. It's a warm feeling, deep down inside me, with an endless flow. It's a ribbon with a glow to it, a golden ribbon with energy flowing through it.

Wayne enlarged on his progress at our next meeting.

I feel much more comfortable about the vehicle. I didn't have the conflict between vehicle and spirit this past week. I've felt more relaxed in making decisions regarding everyday situations.

What do you attribute that to?

I would say it's a result of the work we've been doing. I'm much more aware of how the vehicle tries to get me to operate on the basis of its set notions. I'm much wiser about it and feel more natural about not getting all fired up in relation to its pressures. I can accept the emotions of the vehicle—that overpowering grasp it has to get me to conform to what it thinks. It's spirit growth that has made this possible. Of course, I'm still a novice at handling these forces.

I interpreted Wayne's remark as a signal for me to help him go further. My limited experience in the use of spirit power left unclear how much force I was unleashing. The degree of spirit release had to be compatible with Wayne's capacities. A reasonable solution seemed to be a buddy system.

I hope to use my spirit to expose my vehicle to you—to enter it, look it over, as you have attempted to do with yours. Then I'll report what I see. In that way we can share what we learn for ourselves and from each other by going into our own vehicles.

As soon as I was centered in spirit, I was propelled inward. Awarenesses came, relating to past and present problems—particularly suffering that my vehicle produced, fears and anxieties that stemmed from entrusting myself to the vehicle for care and protection. A large portion of these revelations exposed the vehicle's attempts to manage me. Then spirit-self invited the vehicle to rely more than ever on spirit strength as a basis for deepening inner harmony. I revealed the substance of all this to Wayne, and his reactions were surprisingly similar to the overpowering, flooding sensations that had occurred in past spirit dyads. Yet something more was being catalyzed for him.

My spirit is seeing something deep down within my vehicle, a coconut with a hard shell on the outside, along with very soft material on the inside. The soft part is the core of me. It's the first time the soft part has allowed itself to be exposed like this. It's a very delicate part which could be considered the child inside. The shell is surrounding this part. It feels very comfortable being open with that soft inner substance. There isn't any need to be guarded. Now our spirits are in a vast area together. There is very little difference in relation to each other's spirit and the universe. My vehicle seems to have lost its function. It has no need to hold on to anything in this kind of environment. It doesn't need to gain the upper hand. Now the shell has disappeared. What's appearing underneath looks like a new, white object that has been born within me— or something freshly grown.

An object?

There's no form to it.

This statement of formlessness caused a quivering of my spirit-self. I was inundated with associations of my struggle with the formless pre-belly baby flow. Although I knew that he experienced this newborn something as formless, I asked Wayne if he could add some descriptive material. A minute or so passed.

It has the appearance of something very delicate. It appears to be white in color, something like a rosebud. Now it's moving around a bit to see if it has any movement or freedom. I see two vehicles approaching each other. They are flowing together. It's a different feeling from the one I usually have— when my vehicle is opposing another vehicle. My spirit space can function very well with yours, but it's a new experience for my vehicle to function that well with your vehicle.

How do you mean?

I have the feeling that our vehicles are very similar. In the past, if I got too close to another vehicle, I'd feel a strain, particularly a vehicle with strength like yours. Any powerful vehicle felt like a threat. Most times the other vehicles have had the good sense to stay clear rather than to get on a collision course with mine. It seems to me that this is the problem with practically all vehicles—a power struggle, a matter of insecurity, that shell coated with a hard substance to protect the infant inside.

What do you sense produced that flowing together of our vehicles?

The vast space of the spirit, the feeling that nobody owns it, the sense of having no boundaries, no death struggles, feeling a oneness and a part of the whole universe. I feel a part of it all, especially that tremendous energy that flows through it all. It's the same feeling I had some time ago that scared me. Now, if I want to obtain that energy from the universe, I just bring it in, move it down into my body and it calms me. It's all there for the taking.

I've sensed this feeling for a long time, but I couldn't put my finger on it. I couldn't let it develop and show itself even though I knew something like that was there. I felt it as a small, helpless, defenseless child in many situations. I would immediately stop the feeling and get back behind the hard shell. If that sensitive child can turn to the spirit when it feels threatened, without putting up a wall, it may work out.

Six weeks passed before I heard from Wayne, as he had been away on a number of business trips. I arranged to meet with him the day he called. I had reached positive conclusions regarding his spirit progress, which led to an uneasiness in seeing him again. What if all we had gone through together had been nullified? Vehicular-me was acting up again, demanding reassurance from my spirit, poking fun, implying that maybe my spirit wasn't that wise after all. But the issue was settled immediately after Wayne arrived.

I feel I'm four years older since I last saw you. All of a sudden one part of me seems to have undergone a lot of personal growth and development in a spirit way. The idea of four years is putting a form on it, but it's that little child within me that feels the growth. I've always felt that little, insecure boy there. I still do. But I have a different feeling now, of being able to take care of that self. The universal power I can call on keeps coming into this inner nature and helping it to feel stronger all the time.

It's amazing to me that in six to eight weeks all this has happened to me. I feel more of the totality of things. I see that little white bud quite often—that very tender, sensitive part of me, like a delicate rose with its shell opened up, with the white part of the coconut showing. Whenever I feel uptight, it comes into view, and I can relate to it. This has made a marked difference in my approach to things. The way I was functioning six months ago, compared to now, was so primitive. Back then, I was trying to figure things out. This way is so super, so intelligent, and the results so great. It seems almost unreal. Now I want more of it.

I needed more substantiation regarding Wayne's enthusiasm and pressed him for details, particularly in relation to daily activities and his disturbed feelings in experiencing himself alone.

I still have that feeling about flying by myself. Sometimes my vehicle tries to get me to avoid flying alone by trying to convince me that I'm not up to par physically. I deal with it by saying to the vehicle, You may not feel well, but you aren't sick. I recognize what's going on quickly now. I get in the aircraft, and I see that white thing, and I say to myself, You don't have to be insecure. I breathe and feel the spirit coming in, which seems to disintegrate the jarring force of the vehicle.
I flew today. In the past I'd start to think about the next day's flight. I'd begin to worry about the weather, that sort of thing. I went to bed last night, slept well, without concerning myself how I'd manage

today. I just did what I had to do on the trip today. I filed my flight plan, checked the weather, appraised the whole situation, got in the airplane and took off—without hassling myself. There were some sticky incidents during the flight. I felt a queasiness once or twice being up there all alone, but I also had a good feeling—that I was responsible and could handle it. I didn't have the usual feeling that something awful was going to happen. That didn't register. I was too engrossed in what I was doing.

That spirit feeling is different from day to day. Right now I feel I have it all together, or at least close to that. There is a very relaxed feeling in my abdomen and throughout my body. It feels tremendous. That's why I'm asking, How do I stay in the groove? I know I can't maintain that flow all the time. It gets channelled away. But I don't know how I got to feel this essence. That's the thing. How did I get into my belly? I realize I need to allow myself enough free time to experience myself or risk running into trouble. It's a poor excuse to say I don't have the time to devote to learning how to flow with that spirit space more.

I'm beginning to realize that I have to do more for myself, on my own, to keep the spirit. I guess it's similar to working out physically and exercising my body. If I don't develop my spirit muscles, I know I'm going to continue to have trouble. But the hangup is that I don't know how to apply myself. Maybe it has to do with what works for me—rather than what you've done with me in the past, in trying to help me experience my spirit plane. For example, I was feeling uptight the other day at a peak of mental activity. I didn't know how to get myself out of it. Suddenly, a phrase popped into my head: Let my body go. It felt right. I believe it's a good phrase for me because as soon as I repeated it to myself I had an immediate reaction of relief.

I barely caught my breath before I became aware of the next step. With Lynn and Wayne I'd had a groundwork of knowing them as people and their plights. But now I was prepared to start from scratch with someone—to gain more understanding of the potentials of spirit help.

Paula did not call for an appointment, contrary to accepted protocol for patients. She came to my home unannounced for the purpose of looking me over; but I was unavailable. She then informed my wife that she would know at a glance whether I was the person for her. Novelties are few after years of practice, and I considered Paula's intuitional confidence refreshingly unique.

She later telephoned and arranged for an appointment. When she arrived, she was highly distraught. Despite her outpouring of complaints, it was impossible for me to determine what was really bothering her. I accepted being temporarily stuck that way with her and simply waited. Each visit she would be relieved after pouring out her troubles, but then the pain would quickly overflow again. She was unwilling to commit herself to a schedule, so I saw her for two months on an emergency basis –whenever she couldn't take it anymore. Finally I insisted that if we were to continue, she would have to agree to weekly appointments, which she reluctantly did.

I did not listen to Paula's brooding in a literal sense. Instead, I positioned myself in spirit awareness, where I could experience her essential nature. No doubt

Paula was brainy, but she was also extremely wary of being hurt by others, so that much of her astuteness was wasted in self-protectiveness. Insulating her pain denied her the expression of a deep flow of spontaneous feelings. Despite her inner struggle, she was able to carry on with her job as director of volunteers at a local hospital.

There was a quiet sensuousness that rippled through Paula's youthful, attractive figure. She wore her bronze hair in a ponytail, offsetting a delicate nose and searching, emerald eyes, but it was easy to lose sight of her physical attractiveness in the throes of her distress.

I decided to introduce Paula to the spirit through regular inductive methods, trusting that a gradual saturation in spirit consciousness would become a steadying influence for her. I would have preferred recording our sessions, but Paula was reluctant, so I had her write down her experiences afterwards.

> You were a huge river flowing from strength, coming down the foothills of a mountain. I was a smaller estuary flowing perpendicular to you. My flow moved down a small slope and was finally carried along by your larger flow into a big basin of water which your flow was filling up.

Any doubts I'd had about cultivating an empathetic relationship with her were washed aside by the interconnection she had made, her spirit plane flowing into mine. But my spirit sensed that her feeling of oneness with me indicated more than that, a need to lose herself within my person. To some extent, this appetite for intimacy accounted for her cynical attitude that people used her and took advantage of her need for closeness. Perhaps these thoughts were also going through Paula's mind when she left, obviously upset, with tears streaming down her cheeks. But she had made her first spirit crossing.

Paula had some notes when I saw her the following week, and she used them to refresh her memory.

I felt very sad driving home and cried all the way. But there was no pressure in my head and no head-ache as an aftermath, something I would ordinarily get in going through what we did last time. I found that with a little effort I could direct the pressure down my spine. After about fifteen minutes, what-ever tension remained dropped away. I felt expand-ed inside, along with having a numb-like separate-ness from things around. This really felt good—that I was able to rise above things physically. During the week there was a carryover of calmness. My body seemed to slow down, and I was not bothered as much by situations that might ordinarily annoy me. However, I noticed that as the days wore on, I began to lose the ability to slip into my intimate, quiet place and fell back into feeling tense and un-easy. I have been eager to come here to see you for the past few days. It was as if I was looking forward to finding that purposeful calm and awareness with you that I could not achieve on my own. I felt like a very distinct person, a whole person, separate and important when I left your office last week. Most of my life I've experienced myself as an appendage to others around me, swayed by them.

When Paula first referred to feeling herself as a distinct, important individual, it was difficult for me to relate this to my spirit experiences. The spirit flow was beyond individuality. But as I later reviewed what she had called her numb-like separateness, I realized Paula was referring to being outside her coping plane. She was saying it was a boon not to be dominated by vehicular consciousness, and being free from it gave her an expanded and whole feeling about herself.

Since Paula's baptism into spirit consciousness had been somewhat productive, I attempted another round of spirit contact; but I proceeded cautiously, preferring to build a strong spirit base before going further.

I found myself in a theatre. I couldn't see ahead of me as I entered. There was a large screen up front in place of a stage. I tried to get adjusted to the vastness of the screen. I was pulled into it. A movie came on, depicting a deep space voyage with darkness all around. I was thrust into that galaxy with sunspots exploding. I sensed your presence in that space, too.

I didn't feel as overwhelmed by the experience of our sharing the spirit space as I did the first time we did this. In one respect it was a letdown. I also felt it more in my body than in my head. When we did this last week, my head felt very heavy at first, and it took time for the weight to dissipate. This time my head got heavy at the end as if I wanted to sleep. My arms were tired, too. There were alternating periods of flowing, sometimes while remaining stationary in that space. At other times I experienced your feelings flowing close to or away from mine. I was conscious of a buoyancy during the periods of being in and out of touch with you. When you suggested that I open my eyes after it was over, I felt, No, no—not so soon! I found myself trying to soak up the boundaries of my space, and take it along with me in an invisible net. I kept going back to collect more of what was in that inner space before leaving it, so that I could savor it more.

When I saw her next, she alerted me to her changed mood.

This week I didn't feel anything spectacular in the way of relief or elation. I did notice a deeper quality of relaxation, an almost laissez-faire nonchalance toward living. This went along until three nights ago when I got depressed. I couldn't concentrate on anything except some worrisome thoughts about getting pregnant. I think it was a physical reaction to my ovulation because when I checked the calendar I found I was overdue. I felt better the next day and have since then. But the feelings were ones I have had since I was able to release my negative feelings about the past—namely, that I wanted to scream at my first gynecologist and my ex-husband and tell them all the things I had bottled up within me.

There was an ominous tone in Paula's references to her past, particularly regarding a possible pregnancy. I was tempted to use this festering problem to pry further, as I once would have done; but to pursue it would have pushed Paula into depths of distressing remembrances, and I was now committed to avoiding pockets of negative vehicular feeling. Paula needed a spirit refuge and I needed one as well. Although she perceived me as a flowing river, at times I visualized myself navigating a boat along that river, being bombarded from either shore by both her vehicle and mine. Only by remaining in that freely moving channel, propelled by the flow, could I function in the spirit process.

Paula must have been ruminating too, for she had more to add concerning the delicate balance of positive and negative forces she observed within herself.

> I sense that I will never feel secure in having a baby until I feel purged of the feelings from the past. You can find peace for today, but the rage goes on and on. The bad feelings don't come up as often as they did, but it's predictable that they will come around my menses or during periods of sickness. Then those depressing memories bubble over.

I again diverted Paula's attention from the negative by asking her about her spirit flow in relation to current activities. It took a minute or two for her to shift gears.

> I've had a lot of schedule changes at the hospital, but I've been able to look at them as if they were a problem for someone else—not me personally. Just today, the hospital director revised my work load when I was all set to handle the rounds in the usual way. I was surprised when I didn't become angry.

I did question him about the changes. When he held his ground, I dropped the issue. I felt that this was part of his job. Experiencing these different planes of consciousness must be working because my vehicle is making a lot of noises, challenging the right of spirit-me to be in control.

Despite Paula's inroads to spirit experiencing, I had a strong urge to be on the safe side and establish an even firmer spirit foundation. It was nothing I could put my finger on—just a sensing from spirit awareness. And it proved accurate as our work progressed.

I felt an ebb and flow, in and out of your plane of consciousness, a kind of magnetism drawing me to it. Then, when you spoke, I noticed that my plane moved away. At times I would sense something before you spoke, akin to what you actually said soon afterwards. Toward the end, I felt myself straining to catch your message—for me to lose myself. At that point my consciousness alternated between a tight and restricted feeling between my temples and an expanding feeling deep down in my body. This culminated in an oval ring or knot-hole sensation. It was as if your message—my losing myself—burned into me and made an indelible mark of warmth deep in my abdomen. After I was able to lose myself I moved higher. It was as if I wanted to surround myself in your flow which seemed to be on a lower plane. I could do this only by reminding myself that I was not in my head.

When I let myself move down, I felt a large mass of energy form which eventually became the side of a mountain. The mountainside seemed to go higher from that lower level as if a volcanic eruption was pushing it out of the ground. It was like a tooth erupting. I was drawn closer to the side of the mountain mass and pulled upwards with it. This happened three separate times, each time with a lurch upwards. Finally, I felt myself take a swooping dive, like a bird that soared from one peak to a valley below, then upwards again.

Paula's analogies hinted at a jelling of this phase of our spirit work. Her awareness of my impressions before I voiced them, as well as the indelible mark of warmth deep in her abdomen, suggested an optimum of spirit infusion. With a spirit space to draw on, she seemed ready for more advanced work. I felt this might help to resolve her suffering, and that I should not postpone the move any longer.

Although unaware of the nature of Paula's grief, I was unwilling for her to talk about her painful memories in her usual manner. I preferred to rely on our spirit forces as purging agents. Utilizing the spirit plane in combination with a confessional was an untried venture for me, yet all the elements seemed to fit. I was unwilling also to engage in such a revelatory experience without recording the session, to have the material available for review afterwards. When I explained this to her Paula relented.

Now that you're in your spirit flow, I want you to allow your vehicle to reveal all it can concerning the matter that has been troubling you. Let yourself experience it as if it was happening now. Let whatever is set off, in the way of emotional distress, be absorbed by your spirit. If there's an overload of disturbance your spirit cannot soak up, allow that turmoil to be dissolved into my spirit. Now let your vehicle reveal itself while we remain centered in our spirit spaces.

You seem very far away. My spirit space feels like a Shangri-la, somewhere to escape to rather than a place I might otherwise be, fighting ghosts from the past. It's hard to bring the recollection into the spirit space to look at. It just seems to stay away. Now my spirit space is spreading out into a void. The past doesn't have the power to bother me there. I must be blocking out a great deal. My spirit plane feels so safe and separate from the nightmare I once lived. The trauma seems to be doing everything it can to stay away. I can feel a great sadness now.

Without saying so, I knew she was waiting for me to offer some direction. I again encouraged her to allow the trauma to disclose itself as best she could, whatever the circumstances.

My spirit space is more open now, ready to receive anything coming into it. But there are still apprehensions and misgivings in going from experiencing myself now to what was then. I feel the agony as a tired book, that it would only be a rehash. There is a thick layer of guilt flowing from that terrible thing I did, of wanting to change something that can't be changed.

I continued prodding Paula to allow the vehicle to speak for itself. It was another way of signaling her that I trusted moving on, even if she did not. She accepted my cue with a splurge of words.

It's something I've had to live with since my marriage to Brig, my first husband. I was with him while he was stationed in Korea during his army tour of duty. We had been married three years. Then I had the baby. My life meant nothing, but I had a baby anyway. I was beside myself with fear and turmoil after her delivery. I wanted to scream at the doctor, I can't go home and live with my husband! I began to realize what a stupe I'd been to have become pregnant on purpose, to have given him the child he wanted. It was too late. I was in a foreign country —no help, no nurses, no mother, no neighbors, nobody. I realized that Brig wouldn't take care of me properly even if I went hungry. He didn't feed me, bathe me, help me to the bathroom before the delivery. He just sneered. It suddenly hit me that the stupidest thing I could have done was to please him by giving him that child. But the vehicle made me believe that by giving him what he wanted, he'd be satisfied with me. I tried to be the flawless wife, to help him up the ladder to promotion, to fit in socially at the officer club gatherings. That's the only way I knew how to live. My life was utterly superficial. I had never been allowed to be me. The vehicle had the spirit completely imprisoned.

Paula's thoughts were darting now, as if to avoid the actual trauma. I reminded her of drawing on our spirit spaces and again encouraged her to relive the scene with Brig.

My entire diaphragm is tensing up. Brig wants to rip my ribcage apart. I can feel a hot, searing charge, a tension crystallizing into deep bitterness. Brig is saying, Don't tell on me, don't let them discover that I feel inadequate. He's unclothed now, crouching down in order to hide his body so as not to be seen by others. He's still hiding behind his mask. We have a furtive type of arrangement between us with waves of blackness enveloping the area. I'm being pulled into this whirlpool as if drawn by a magnet, having to do things his way. I don't have to think for myself. My eyes have blinders over them. There's a thick rubber band tightening around my temples, synchronized with his philosophies. I feel complete emptiness while I'm waiting for him to do something. It's as if I don't have any purpose in living except when I'm told how to live. I don't dare want something for myself. I feel like a child looking for a lost father, needing to agree with him so that he won't go away.

Now my vehicle is saying that it's supposed to be that way— to justify the marriage and to provide for my survival. I don't want it to be that, but it's a necessary evil. It's very much a game—how much can I sponge off him before he turns on me and tries to sponge off me. I find it suffocating. Now there's a band around my chest. He wants to control everything so he can say he's in charge. He's afraid to do some things, but he's also driven to accomplish them to prove something to himself.

He has to maintain an image of being somebody important through his achievements. He doesn't care if people get mad at him as long as he eventually gets his way. He likes the big scene to show that he's all man. He keeps complaining that I'm not there for him, to clean, to cook, to sleep with him—the things all the wives of the other officers are capable of doing. I don't have the stamina to keep going. I feel myself crushed. The easiest thing to do is to give in so as to have peace.

Paula stopped speaking momentarily. I asked her what was wrong. She said she had to back away a bit from the unbearable stress she was experiencing. I invited her to let her spirit draw on mine for replenishment. When she resumed I noticed that she was reliving the situation in the past tense—as if immersion, as a current experience, was too overwhelming.

After the baby was born, I didn't want Brig sexually anymore. It was as if the last vestiges of feeling for him had been ruined, a closed chapter. I was faced with a situation in which every single day was repulsive to me. I wanted something to manipulate too. I could no longer accept being completely under his heel. But my vehicle was no match for his vehicle. As soon as I'd become physically exhausted, he'd treat me worse than ever and take advantage of my weakened condition to manipulate my mind and my body as well.
I felt somewhat relieved when he was away on maneuvers. Still I couldn't face the fact that I might not have him there at all. It was like living a

nightmare with a time bomb set to go off. I was unable to speak up. When I did, he ridiculed me. The vehicle kept wanting to destroy the baby all during those weeks after leaving the hospital. I heard my spirit saying, No! You can't! The vehicle kept thinking, You've got to do it; you've got to get it over with, to hurt him so that he won't be able to deny your rage toward him. I had an advance warning. During the delivery I freaked out. I saw the beginning of the end coming, a terrible fear and depression, a wild animal taking over, wanting to smash, scream, yell, pound people's heads against the wall, to tell them they had to listen to me. There was a terrible apprehension that I'd be unable to control myself. But every time I was on the verge of crying out they'd tell me to shut up.
By the time the baby was six weeks old, the situation was completely chaotic. Brig had night duty on a military exercise. I was afraid to tell him what I felt. I couldn't face the truth—that I wanted to kill my child. I didn't dare let her out of my sight. I felt that with enough willpower and determination I could get through the crisis. But it all began to give way. I decided to do the thing that night when the baby was asleep, when she wouldn't know anything. I got up at five in the morning, walked over to the crib, took a pillow and smothered her. I murdered my own baby.

I was stunned. I was caught off guard by the impact of this revelation. Paula was crying hysterically, yet there was an underlying something that seemed to be calming her. I interpreted this as the spirit force providing a degree of absolution from her suffering. I encouraged Paula to allow both of our spirit spaces to saturate her deepest feelings. We sat in silence while she collected herself before continuing.

I really hit him where it hurt. He was unable to function for days afterwards. The idea of destroying the child was completely beyond any conception he ever had of me or anybody in this world. But I finally blew his cool to the extent that he became unglued. Of course, I was totally wiped out at that point. But I had gotten back at him. I had expressed the ultimate, an irreversible intent to get rid of him and to show him that I couldn't stand what he was doing to me. I was convinced I was setting myself up to be destroyed in a gas chamber. It didn't work out that way because I was declared to be crazy. In the back of my mind I had surrendered my will to this one act—once it was over my life would be finished too. Afterwards, I was a thing waiting to be delivered to the courts. He was utterly shattered. He realized for the first time how much I really hated him, that it wasn't the baby that was the target of my rage, but him. Now he could see that he had done things that would have made me violent enough to kill. I was glad that it was over, out in the open, that I didn't have to pretend anymore about us. I was glad that I had found his Achilles heel, that he couldn't fight back. I knew he could never have been reached unless it was a powerful blow. Even though I was out of my mind, the fact that I couldn't have asked for professional help at the time really stunned me. I kept thinking to myself after it was over, Why doesn't he hit me or kick me? All he wanted to do was to yell for help. It was then that I realized he was vulnerable and human after all.

Even though there was little left of my spirit, glimmerings of a tender side of myself were also present. I remember the moments I held the baby, and she smiled and focussed her eyes when I put my finger to her nose. It was my spirit sharing itself with hers. I felt alive then, aware, able to do anything, a sense of realness, a purpose for living. But then it vanished just like the things I enjoyed as a child in relation to nature, a kindly feeling toward animals, singing in the choir. They all went down the drain with Brig. But in order to keep going, I knew I had to have someone stronger than I was. I figured that Brig could take care of me. I never conceived that it would turn out the way it did. But that's all I knew, that I was supposed to give in to a husband, like it was the law of the land, part of the biblical code.

If I hadn't been so drawn to Brig sexually, if I hadn't lived off sex the way I did with him, I might not have stayed married all that time. I was strongly attracted to him physically, to his body. It was a tremendous release to have him overwhelm me sexually. I had slept with a lot of men, but nothing compared to what I had with him. I suppose it meant a lot to his manhood to have been able to get me to respond to him in the lustful way I did. But he was almost Machiavellian in his efforts to use that to subordinate me to his will. If that kind of sex hadn't been there, I couldn't have tolerated continuing to live with him. I would have spent more time looking at what was going on instead of being so completely sucked into the vortex.

I needed to catch my breath as a result of this avalanche of vehicular pain Paula had unleashed at my spirit consciousness. I momentarily redirected Paula's attention to factual information.

What happened after you killed the baby?

I was sent back to the United States immediately and admitted to a psychiatric hospital near Baltimore, close to home. Since the murder took place in a foreign country, it was up to the military to decide my fate. The army chose not to prosecute. They considered me mentally incompetent at the time I did it.

And after that?

I remained in the hospital for a year and a half. I saw a staff psychiatrist in therapy three times a week for the first six months and twice weekly for the remaining year. Brig filed for divorce during my stay at the hospital. By that time the medical evaluation showed that I was ready for discharge. I continued to see the same psychiatrist privately for two more years. I married Ron three years later.

Being centered in the spirit space while hearing the tail end of Paula's revelation was a strange experience for me. I was without any moral judgment concerning her actions. My vehicle would have had censuring attitudes and feelings, but being one with spirit consciousness left me free to continue with equanimity. Since I doubted whether our effort had expurgated the full measure of Paula's deep-seated guilt, I asked Paula to let herself silently absorb as much of my spirit consciousness as she could. After several minutes of vibrational flow, she picked up the thread of our joint experience.

I can live in the spirit. I know I can. I see myself as that spirit forgiving my vehicle—with a chance for dignity and grace, a new birth and a clean slate, not controlling or being controlled, as a spirit self. I sense a concern for the vehicle, the source of too much suffering for too long. The vehicle wanted something better. It wanted a release and knew only one way—to escape, or to have others put the vehicle away in an institution where it could no longer be trapped in an impossible existence. The spirit can be a counterbalance to the vehicle. To be wholly free, the vehicle must give way to the spirit —to listen to it and share.

Let's take a few minutes and let our spirit spaces experience a depth of silence, a spirit release and reverence for the vehicle's past sufferings, a sense of new possibilities for both the spirit and the vehicle. See if you can let that stillness flow and inundate past agonies. Allow your spirit plane to flow into mine and let it absorb as much as it wants to in a restorative way.

Thus, with my spirit force at its fullest capacity, I offered a kind of benediction, going beyond anything I had ever previously envisioned sharing with a patient. There was a detumescence of surface stirring as the quietness took hold. I was aware of an extra dimension of spirit interflow. Paula broke the extended quietness with a rush of impressions.

I really felt like an outsider while we were doing this. There was a sense of real pity for the vehicle, for the person I used to be. I could see it from a distance. That happened more in the beginning and particularly in the middle as the process evolved. It was only at the end that I felt overwhelmed by the grief of the vehicle. I was on another plane at times. I felt sadness for the vehicle, that it had to go through this sort of thing. I could sense the spirit there as a separate entity. It was very comforting to have it as a buffer. I didn't feel like I was completely surrounded or controlled by the grief. The spirit space was a protection from that. I had this concern for the vehicle, like I would for another person who had lost their family or someone dear to them, like they had hurt themselves and I didn't want that to happen. But the time lag, the time space, the dispassionate sense I had was different from times past when I might have wanted to tear my hair. It was as if I could feel with another person yet not be so completely inundated by their sorrow that it might make it impossible to function. I could still hold on to my spirit while all of this was being seen. It was very important to me that I could feel all of this. At times the spirit space would get narrower, crowded or pressured, but I felt it there all the time. I felt the quietness move out to me, the stillness going back and forth between our spirit spaces, first pulling a little toward me and then flowing back toward you. I wanted to grab you toward the last, to grip your hands and pull myself up from the pit, or have you reach out and pull me on to an island, an oasis. I felt I was at the end of my rope. Not until then did I really feel the spirit force and soak up your spirit power and mine.

Also, it was my ability to use the spirit as a spotlight that really helped—to focus on the pain within me, the suffering from the past. I was controlling that spotlight, no one else. I was not in the light, but behind it, where I could feel safe. It was comparable to tapping the source of the universe by making that spotlight work the way I wanted it. I was able to see what was really there, in the light, clearly and with-out bias, and to feel a trust in doing that. Myths thrive on darkness and shadows. In staring into the past that way, I could slide down the beams of light and get close to the situation and not feel that I was being swallowed up by it. I felt I was involved with what I was seeing, and yet safe, because I was drawing on the ability of the spirit observer to look at it.

Formerly, I would have tried to understand, or at least classify, Paula's violent act. But now, knowing why she did such a thing was academic. I was not engaged in a cause-and-effect analysis of her problem. Instead, I saw her awakening spirit as capable of releasing her from unresolved suffering. Through all of this I was impressed by the help the spirit had provided, something I, as professional-me, never could have offered.

Previously, I had never considered confession a particularly helpful device for self-renewal. But this was a view held by my secular consciousness, which was incapable of providing expurgation for its own mischief. It was clear that contrition required dispensation from a spirit plane, beyond the reaches of the vehicle's domain. Moreover, if Paula's spirit was capable of such purification, perhaps it could also help to resolve other areas of her suffering.

She had specific things to say in that regard when she returned.

> I felt a lot better during part of the week. I didn't expect the experience to release me from the trauma to such an extent. It was as if a huge load had been lifted from my back, and for two days afterwards I felt like a new person, like a door had been slammed shut on the past for good. But as soon as the grief and the guilt of the last session left, something else hit me like a ton of bricks. I hadn't been aware that my marriage to Ron had been haunting me that much, that I'd done it to myself all over again with a second husband.

Exposing the pretenses of her relationship with Ron would have been helpful if Paula had been inclined to use her spirit consciousness to examine her vehicle's maneuverings. But as I listened I realized that Paula remained determinedly self-righteous. I shuddered at this, not only for Ron's sake, but for what it implied for me.

For many weeks there was no letup in her frantic bid to rearrange her marriage. Her acrimony toward Ron was a familiar and well-worn attempt to dump her unhappiness on him: he was completely at fault. At times her anger was subtly directed at me as well. It seemed she was holding me partly accountable for the unwelcome realization. At one point she decided that I should see Ron—to help him become the kind of person who could make the marriage work. I was helpless to satisfy her need, and told her so.

With no immediate solution in sight, her mental activity took over, flooding her with quick remedies. But her desperate efforts only caused greater confusion. In many ways I hadn't the foggiest notion what I could do other than to draw her out.

I know he must have a problem. How could anyone in his late twenties only want to take me to bed once a week? I'm the one who invariably has to approach him, the one who will kiss him passionately, who will tap him on the shoulder in the middle of the night to make love. I don't want to have to teach him the ways he should touch me and love my body. I want him to know that for himself. He's not loose, not free. Only if he's stone drunk, off on a vacation or viewing some porno movie does he get aroused. If I have to fight with him to get him to want me, it just isn't worth it. It's no fun feeling alone when you're with someone physically. I want it to be a flowing of the mind as well as the spirit. I want to be able to get a reciprocal response from him.

Was it different before you married him?

We did share our philosophies and thoughts when we first met. But there was no sexual involvement. Since he was a virgin, I reasoned that he had to have a great respect for sexual proprieties, that he would be a good sex partner later on. I wasn't eager to rush into that kind of precious and beautiful experience with him anyway. I found out with Brig what it was like to be married to someone's good looks and body without having the compassion and kindness to go with it. Furthermore, Ron was sensitive and intelligent. He also took religion seriously and, with my own strong interest in the church, there seemed every reason to believe that we would find a spirituality with each other.

When I didn't offer any solution to the impasse with Ron, Paula was left to deal with it on her own. She still seemed to be waiting for my reaction when she casually mentioned that there was an intern at the hospital who had dropped by her office at odd times. Her attempt to explain Brandon seemed a way of selling me, as well as herself, on his value to her as a friend.

There's such an aliveness in him that Ron lacks. Some people seem to have much more intensity. Brandon asked me to have coffee with him the other day. I felt all charged up inside me when he touched me on the elbow. It hit me that I hadn't had any exciting contact like that in the two years I've been married to Ron.

Paula continued to drop a word here and there regarding her brief but stirring encounters with Brandon. Several weeks later she confided to having slept with him.

I had a good cry at home during the week. The recurring thought was in regard to my father, how he wanted so much for me to be able to do my own thing. I really felt his loneliness and could sense the alienation he had to life. I knew he didn't want that for me. The feeling I got from him was, Don't waste it.

Seeing Brandon pushed me into more of what I remembered with my father. Brandon is such a strong, vigorous, physical person. There he was dangling the apple in front of my face. I didn't want to look at it. I was afraid it might be another vortex. Still I was intrigued by what was out there. Yet, another part of me didn't want to know, so I had to go tippy-toe around to see what kind of personality he had. We had quite a discussion as to how each of us felt about ourselves and about people. He was able to tell me what he liked in another person. He wanted to come and go in the relationship and not be held down or held back. I was able to tell him some of the things I felt were important to me. Neither of us wanted to play games. I'm glad I went to bed with him. Now I don't feel so possessed by the desire of having wanted him. He said, Good, I hope you don't flip over me.

Before I was extremely tense around him, being the kind of physical animal he is. He'd send out all kinds of low-key sexual messages. It's the first time I've had sex with anybody else while being married, either time. I was glad because it freed me from being hung up on the idea. I felt a tremendous relief because I needed to share him, and I couldn't see beyond that. It was the best sex I've had since Brig. The whole lid came off for me when I said I felt he was a person I could grow with both mentally and emotionally. I didn't feel so alone when I discovered how much he needed intensity and feedback, too. It meant a lot that I didn't have to sit around wishing for something out there. I could do it, get it, and not be possessed by it.

The euphoria was bound to end. When it did, she was left with Ron once more—someone who would always be there, just as her mother had been. And despite her highs and lows with Ron and Brandon, Paula continued to realize more spirit.

My vehicle doesn't want to move over for spirit-me. I've been biding my time to get through this week, to get back to where I can just be that spirit-me. Otherwise, the only way I've been able to manage is to jump into the spirit space and look at the world from a loving, I-don't-care attitude—just feeling the spirit, watching life go by. It's similar to being in a space where no one can hurt me. Still, what do I do when I have to cope all day long at the hospital? I can't stay in the spirit flow forever. The spirit may want to look at the scenery, and I have to keep my eyes on the road.

Are you saying that the spirit force is separate and apart from your daily life, that there is no flow of your spirit into your involvements?

There isn't much of a flow. There's a definite, concerted effort on my part to keep the spirit plane going. But it's not like the spirit force has taken over and is running things. I haven't really learned enough or felt enough to let the quiet space spill over the other way, into the forms of my life. I can feel the calmness and enjoy it, but it's still very segregated.

I've been having a hard time staying in the spirit space. It's difficult for me to handle both the vehicle and the spirit. I feel cut up.

What do you sense about this?

I've allowed the impasse with Ron to take hold of me, as if I have to prove that I'm capable of handling the problem. The vehicle feels it's got to assure itself that it can cope, that it can work the issue through to a logical conclusion, find the facts and come to a rational answer.

The vehicle seems to have a picture of what it has to accomplish and achieve to be successful.

My vehicle feels it has to achieve certain results to justify its existence. It feels depressed at times, not knowing how it will fit into a life where it's obliged to share the space of the spirit force. Until recently, I would only feel terror when I thought I was going over the edge, no longer able to cope. It's the same fear that I've had regarding losing face—that I'll have nothing left of me, nothing to hang on to.

The last session tended to cement more of a oneness relationship with the spirit space. I was much freer, felt much calmer, things didn't bug me during the week. I felt some misgivings about being a nonperson—what I really mean is a non-doing person. The fact that I was not as involved in thinking about what I should be doing worried me once in a while, and I had a recurring question: What am I supposed to be? But I wasn't excited about anything. I found that I stayed on an even keel. This was a new experience. It was a great leveller and really felt good. Ron still couldn't perform, but I didn't get uptight about it. I figured, Well, I've got my own satisfactions. I didn't feel like running away from him. Whatever frustrations came along during the week were like mosquitoes that went away after awhile. I thought it was kind of strange to be on an even keel all the time—no ups or downs, no getting involved, no getting mad or being happy. It was sort of a neutral zone. But it wasn't empty. I had the fear that I might feel nothing or that being in that spirit zone like that might be a washout, a namby-pamby existence, a flat potato without salt or pepper. I said to myself, Hang on a little longer and see if this is going to be the case. It proved not to be. Then the spirit would settle out, and there would be a lot of depth to it. It was a new kind of experience for me, the sense of an inner core and an expanding outward trip.

What came to me is that the spirit is not a marshmallow. It's a real, dynamic, strong, creative, explosive force. I asked myself, Are you going to recognize it or not? I know that calls for a certain commitment.

Paula's discovery of that neutral spirit space in daily activity allowed me to feel freer about taking a month's vacation. She must have noted my concern, because she quickly reminded me that she would manage quite well on her own.

When we resumed, I found my concern regarding Paula's ability to manage for herself during my absence had been indeed unwarranted.

The spirit space was the one thing that kept me going. I found myself turning back to it for strength on numerous occasions. I've discovered, however, after tapping into the spirit flow, that a certain amount of time has to elapse for me before things fall into place. I have to experience what the spirit is telling me in one situation after another before I can accept it as being true.

My spirit life during the past weeks could be compared to the Panama Canal with its intricate dike system. I'd go into one lock within myself and get filled up with the spirit flow on that level. Then I'd go into another and the spirit force would flood that one. I've been watching the different spaces fill up and accepting each breakthrough as it has occured. Apparently that's the way my body is geared to integrate the spirit. Since I've stored my feelings and emotions in different enclosures all my life, it takes time for the spirit to seep and ooze into all of those little compartments. It will take even more time for the spirit flow to reach the gut level.

Undoubtedly, Paula had made an important thrust into spirit consciousness. However, to join her in a bit-by-bit clearing of her vehicle would be piecemeal decompartmentalization, incompatible with the total, free release of spirit. I felt more keenly than ever that I had to maintain my spirit integrity.

I asked Paula to give me a few minutes for quiet centering, preferring not to engage in any discussion until I could allow more spirit force to build within me. Various impressions began to form. Until now, I had permitted her to draw on my entity and presence to gain a spirit foothold, but it was time for her to shed that dependency on my person and rely on the cosmic spirit flow.

> It's important that you experience me, not as the physical person I appear to be, but as spirit. We're going to return to the beginning of your spirit being, prior to your

*physical conception, to give you a chance to be born as
spirit. To do that you'll need to surrender your awareness
of all forms, gradually slipping back in time prior to your
conception. At that point, I want you to allow all consciousness of form to disappear. Then enter my space, a
place where I am totally formless, as a spirit being. You
are to lose yourself as completely as possible in my
formless field and flow. If you conceptualize anything
regarding your physical birth within my spatial environs,
allow that to occur. You originated from formlessness,
from a flow of energy particles and life-forces that congealed into your form. Your essence has a formless quality.*

I can see where the sperm and the ovum have
physical form at that point.

See if you can surrender to entering my space.

I have already.

*I'm going to give you an extended period of time to live
out whatever comes to you as I remain centered in my
spirit flow.*

Finally, Paula broke the stillness.

It took a while for the spirit flow to come to me.
Then I remembered my mother baking cookies for
me as a child. I could sense a release as you said
for the infant spirit-me to enter your spirit space.
There was water bubbling in your flow, much as I
experienced some time back. Then you said for me
to be born again, and I felt my human shape dis-

solve with the spirit filling out to the edges of that cookie dough. Yet I did not become limp. I could feel my muscles and bones, but they weren't the major element. It was more that the musculature was a house for the spirit to live in, to fill out and to have its place there.

I was about to ask Paula to repeat this excursion, but she suddenly became fatigued. The attempt to reconnect her to a nascent spirit life was more taxing for her than I had anticipated, so I waited until she was able to continue.

Immerse yourself in my spirit space once again. You're about to come into this world as form and spirit. Just as you're leaving my space, as part of a birth process, you become aware of a congregation of people in our midst. They have a deep appreciation of their inner spirit and the cosmic spirit. Passing you from one person to another, they take you in their arms and embrace you. They are a welcoming committee. As they hold you, rock you, and comfort you, they are expressing their delight regarding your arrival in form. But while sharing that, they don't want you to lose track of your dependence on the formless renewing process. Breathe this spirit process and let it replenish your strength. Let it supply you with that formless energy as if it were a spirit parent, feeding the depths of your inner spirit, at the core of your belly, as you share your spirit life with us. You may feel, at times, that your spirit is in touch with ours, knowing that we are all dependent on the formless surround for sustenance and renewal of both our form and formless selves.

Once I got myself into focus, I didn't need your space any more.

That's right. You don't need my presence once you've made a direct connection to the pure spirit.

It takes time to pull out spirit energy.

You'll notice that your vehicle finds it hard to wait and is very impatient.

Once it happens, though, it's an unusual sensation. I notice my body tingling, the skin feeling stirred from an energy source, a soulful depth to it.

The depth can be felt as touching the source of spirit essence. If you don't realize the depth, you may feel starved in relation to spirit nurturing.

Yes, a kind of spirit anemia, that's true. Then the vehicle steps in to fill the void. I can see that now.

If you don't retain that spirit source within you, you fail to provide an essence foundation for yourself.

That's what I must get through my head--that I need to depend on that basc, rather than on what other people tell me.

What anybody tells you comes under the heading of form.

I just had a feeling of something—that I never cut

the cord with my mother. I've only separated from her intellectually and have never gone beyond.

Your form-to-form dependency on your mother would have to leave you stuck. There's only so much power you can obtain from her restricted form before it runs down.

I can see where that kind of dependency would become exhausting for both of us. Like a breathing system for divers, it's only good for a certain number of hours. Somehow there should be a formless essence there. I guess I'd describe it as freewheeling, a flowing back and forth.
I guess it's like the kid who puts his hand in the river. He doesn't need to be told, Now you're going to experience the flow, the coolness, the texture. He doesn't need to get a lecture on what it is. He just needs to dive in and Whoopee! He's there.

Let the spirit course through you more fully; let it firm your backbone, your spinal column. Allow it to impregnate all your muscle fibres to release your spirit strength.

I spoke with my mother recently about this, that I grew up feeling that I shouldn't assert myself, that I should be nice to people, that I was put on earth to help others. She couldn't understand why I should have felt that way. It really doesn't matter how I came to it. I can't go back and change what happened. The fact is that I was crippled by the fear of being myself, the fear of using my strength.

She was saying she couldn't assert herself, but the kind of asserting she was referring to was based on a vehicular orientation. Paula could not comprehend spirit assertion until she released its power in actual practice.

If you only conceive of yourself as form, living within the confines of your vehicle, what is it that you sense if you consider asserting yourself?

Limitations! I get tired and hungry; the muscles feel as if they're wearing out as my body breaks down.

If you allow yourself to be born as spirit, feeling a connectedness to that source, what do you experience if you assert yourself from that spirit domain?

I don't picture myself acting forcefully that way either. I feel like a capsule floating down a river, just enjoying the scenery by myself. I don't see anybody else but me.

If I'm relating to you from my spirit, there's an openness throughout my body. I'm not thinking of anything. I'm free of all forms. That means I'm encountering you at a point where I'm clear, without bias, devoid of all emotion, preconception or prior conditioning. Then I allow the spirit to begin unfolding. The beginning of that is a sense of flow in the depths of my abdomen, which in time begins to be felt as a oneness with everything formless—all the unformed energy and life-force that exists. I can absorb the formless energy through the breathing, allowing it to invade the depths of my being. When I turn to relate to you, I retain as fully as I can the sense of that total flow within my spirit space. Only after I've realized that core feeling do I allow the awareness of your presence into my consciousness. I maintain freedom from forms that might develop from the neck up—thereby preventing the vehicular mentality from grabbing that energy, taking over, and churning up all kinds of unreal programs. As long as I maintain quietness in my head, permitting forms to occur in the lower half of my body, I depend on my spirit center.

You've lost me again.

Form comes from formlessness. Forms are merely congealed, circumscribed fields of what previously were formless life-forces and energies.

Then what?

If I depend on that spirit source, with its formless energy, at the base of my inner essence, I'll be plugged into the totality of formlessness. I'll be ready to receive forms arising from that vast formless energy flow. If forms generate from that spirit base, as a result of my connectedness with it all, I'll feel the ultimate oneness with everything before I even relate to you. I can then relate myself to your form, or any form, from that spirit field which is now impregnated within my belly. It's the essence of sufficiency, integrated with it all, even before becoming involved with parts of it all. Also, I'm free, in a free field. I'm not stuck with my vehicular mentality figuring out how I can be free with all of the piecemeal, intellectual forms I devise to create the illusion of freedom. I have the essence of freedom because, on that spirit plane, there is nothing other than the freedom that accrues from being part of a total and boundless field of formlessness.

Having said this I felt much freer with Paula. She was grinning when she spoke.

I'm amused because I hear the vehicle saying to me, The only way you can be freed from your boxed-in feeling is if people around you are different, if they allow you to be free.

That's the rationalization of the vehicle. It can't help you or handle the problem of freedom for you, so it tries to con you.

I know—it's a con game, pure and simple. I notice that it also steps in to try and fill the emptiness I feel.

We learn to depend on the vehicle very early to fill us up with something, anything that will appease and pacify that emptiness.

The form has to have something, to do something, to be active—isn't that true?

The trouble with that kind of activity is that it produces that foaming and churning in your head. The more it tries to act as a substitute for the essence of you in your belly, the less fulfillment you get in the depths of your spirit.

Right. I haven't trusted relying on those forms that come from below.

You haven't taken advantage of using that essence-forming process in activity to that extent.

I was sitting here thinking that the spirit plane only belonged in the lotus position.

Your coping consciousness doesn't want the spirit force invading its premises, where it maintains control over the activity.

It has only allowed me a bit of titillation. I could sit and enjoy only what it considered acceptable.

If you begin to trust more of that essence base, tied to that spirit process, you give it room to be muscular.

I'm also wondering what happens to those forms afterwards.

Forms are always expendable. They have a life expectancy. Eventually they dissolve back to where they came from, back to the ocean of formlessness, which is an eternal energy flow. That's why formlessness is felt to be ever-present to the nervous system. On that plane of consciousness, the ocean of formlessness is always present.

When you said, Being reborn in the spirit flow, did you mean plugging into that?

Not quite. That comes after the fact. The first considera-

tion is to stay centered in spirit within yourself, letting that alignment produce a regeneration of creative forms arising from the formless, reproductive spirit process. It's like being on the edge of creation and allowing a continuing flow of spirit forms to be delivered.

Is that what you meant by growth of the spirit-self?

You're born only once as the distinct physical form you exist as now. But you can be reborn, regenerated countless times as a spirit being.

Then you're saying that rebirth is an accumulation of spirit forces that have built up within you, that the forces find a direction once they're allowed to accumulate on that base level. By letting that formless spirit flow develop through experiential waiting, the essence of that has to eventually do something of and by itself, which means that the contained energy bursts forth in a birth process—like physical birth.

Yes, only in this instance it's the birth of the spirit.

My attempt to find new ways to awaken Paula's spirit power set me thinking. There was only one course—to take her into herself, as I had done with Wayne. This would entail drawing on her spirit plane to invade the vehicle's stronghold.

What we're confronted with is whether you can strengthen your spirit. It's unlikely that you'll break free of the controls of your structured-self until you develop a more available spirit source. But your progress depends on being less influenced by the vehicle's intimidations.

I suppose I haven't been with sensitive people for long enough periods of time for the spirit to sink in deeply enough.

You don't need to depend on other people to turn on your spirit. If you believe otherwise, you will forever be pulled back to them, depending on their forms, incurring another cycle of suffering.

I knew I sounded categorical, but I recognized that Paula still wanted help from personal-me and I was unwilling to make any further concessions to her entrenched dependency pattern. She reacted half-innocently.

You mean that there's a point where you don't need other people?

For your spirit essence.

I'll have to convince my vehicle about that.

You don't have to convince the vehicle about anything. You simply learn to center yourself, free of the vehicle's controls. The vehicular consciousness, with its set ideas, tends to keep the spirit life mummified. When this produces a state of malnourishment for you, your vehicle attempts to obtain a handout of flow from others.

That's true. I find myself doing that little trick,

relying on other people as hosts so I can be the parasite to those who'll do it with me. I get sucked into it.

Sucked into it?

Well, let's say I've allowed myself to get sucked into the maneuvering.

The danger is that you may continue to harbor the notion that those other forms have denied and deprived you, rather than acknowledge that it's your vehicular mentality which has tied up the energy, will, and wisdom that would ordinarily be there for the spirit plane.

It's been hard for me to contend with people who disagree with me. I become passive whenever I'm in that position. It's been a way of trying to get along with them, I suppose.

Paula's last statement was an attempt to skirt the issue. I decided to intensify our spirit involvement.

Pull in as much spirit power as you can. When you feel it to be at maximum strength, zero in on your vehicle, and explore your form.

It feels like the spirit has been trapped for so long that it's afraid to get near the vehicle. When you said for me to go into my form, a tractor appeared and shoved a stone buttress up against my spirit force. It was saying, So you want to go into the vehicle, do you? See if you can keep from being plowed under.

Then I saw the spirit hovering over it, like a bird on a branch, looking down at a cat, eyeing its predator with a certain security as long as it was out of its grasp. The buttress barrier turned over on its side suddenly and became an empty elevator shaft, an abyss with nothing under it. It was as if I was in an observation car. I was up toward the top observing the shaft open up. The bottom was falling out and the shaft was going down to the depths. I had the idea that someone had dug an excavation and was removing a cover to show what they had done. I couldn't get into the shaft. If I could, I would have slid right down into the spirit space. So I said to myself, Find a tall building and get on an elevator; press the button and go down.

And did you?

I didn't go all the way down at first. Then you said something, and I went right on down. There was no shaft, no obstacle after that. I could feel the spirit flow settle all the way to the bottom and spread out. Going down all the way was similar to the experience I had when you had me enter your spirit space in order to be born again. It was another way of letting go, very much like coming to the bottom of a slide at a playground. It was as if I knew my feet were going to make it all right, and I didn't need to grab hold of anything along the way to keep from stumbling or falling. Once I overcame the fear of sliding down, and a concern about looking ridiculous, it was fun doing it. I felt bigger inside afterwards, more space to be me. Having been in that space before, I was able to click in and say, As long as I'm here, I'm not crushed or caught in the undertow of the pressure the vehicle can put on me. My vehicle was acting like a big bully. At first I felt that my spirit would get flattened or swallowed up if it got inside my form. My vehicle was saying, You think you can handle me? I'm bigger than you are. Toward the last I had the strong impression that my spirit, at the bottom of the shaft, had been there all the while, already dug out, even before I made an effort to get to it.

Paula's elation mounted as she expressed appreciation for my continued support. Again, I felt an aversion to the confidence she placed in personal-me.

I don't think you need me as much as you think you do. You only need to discover how you can tap that spirit which you surmise has been there all your life. If I buy the idea that I'm so valuable to you, then I have to keep supporting an image of indispensability. My vehicle might enjoy the titillation, but my spirit can't submit to that kind of egotism.

She was startled by my assertiveness, and was concerned whether she could handle by herself suffering resulting from long-standing problems.

Suffering is an unnecessary element in one's life. The spirit flow doesn't allow for it. If suffering exists, it's only to the extent the vehicle predominates. All you need do to test the truth of what I'm saying is to put your spirit to work.

You can't imagine what it means to me when you say that the spirit, in its purity, is a way of being free from ordinary suffering. You're really saying, How much pain do you want to bear? You don't have to suffer if you don't want to. As much effort as you give to the spirit is as much freedom from suffering that you'll get back.

I want you to allow yourself to sink into the depths of your spirit source once more and reenter your vehicle. After reaching that stage as spirit, allow the flow to recycle within you.

I can feel myself bobbing around, from the diaphragm level. It's as if I'm in a pool of water. It's settling down a little more now.

Each time you draw in spirit energy, let it sink down as far as the flow will take you. See if you can experience this without form. Allow it to unfold as pure, raw, unformed energy. If something does form above the navel, let it float away, like balloons filled with helium. Stay at that spirit source; let the sensations go deeper within your belly. You may notice that occasionally the formlessness has descended a bit more; if that happens, just accept it. Continue to draw in the formlessness to enhance the flow of energy that goes down that hollow cavity.

I'm in the position of seeing the spirit in the caricature of a dance, and I'm observing its movement.

You'll notice that if you stay centered in your belly and vibrate with the open, formless space of that abdominal chamber, you'll be in a vibrational flow that can set off a certain play, the equivalent of a dance.

As you were talking, I felt a sinking down after I'd gone into the formlessness, like a plane dropping several thousand feet into an air pocket. I let myself soak up the descending movement with its sense of nothingness. Then I heard my vehicle say, No! No! You can't go on that way, you've got to deal with the world as I deal with it!
But it wasn't the hellish low that I thought it might be. It was a great feeling to be in the spirit flow on that base line. I could see I didn't have to stop doing things because of it, that I'd simply approach things from a new point of view. The vehicle has had me hassled with the fear that being taken over by the spirit force would mean living apart from everything and everyone.

As if you'd be ripped away from all form.

Right! It was that kind of nonsense. I was into a holding position, between the vehicle and the spirit planes, and you picked it up. I knew I wanted to get back into the spirit flow. So I pushed the vehicle away and off I went. I realize that my spirit has a special ability. It has expanded my awareness of me. It's as if I have another dimension, a new entity of my being. It's like knowing that my spirit flow has a place in the order of things, that it really has a purpose, a place in the universe. If I'm experiencing natural spirit-me, as a novice, then I must have considerable capacity that way.

It seems to be very reaffirming for you.

Even more than that, I'm feeling a powerful release right now, of tremendous omnipotence, as if I'm invulnerable. I hesitated to use the word *omnipotence* because it might be interpreted as being pretentious. But it's more that I feel I'm drawing on the entire universe.

If a person didn't understand the difference between vehicular and spirit power, it might be misconstrued.

It only lasted for fifteen or twenty seconds.

That's the potential power of the formless spirit flow that you're obliged to deal with.

It wasn't a gentle force. My feeling of omnipotence was raw. I didn't feel like boasting about it. It was just a statement of fact, more like the strength of a charged-up bull.

All you need to remember is that spirit omnipotence springs from a source which is beyond you or me in a vehicular sense.

More importantly, what we did showed me that the spirit can produce forms in and of itself. I hadn't really experienced that until now, even though we've gone over it before. That means the spirit has a special power, something I hadn't realized. It's as strong a force as the vehicle's, even though the forms that the spirit produces are changing continually. Still, I'm wondering how this might affect my relationships with people.

It becomes indispensable when you're involved with others to remain separate and apart from a dependence on their forms. Your detachment permits you to be connected to the spirit recycling process first—at ground-zero, or a point of readiness for the movement of the dance to take place. You then relate to others from that base line. Then you learn—not from them, but about them, about life, about everything—from your essence source. So you're not dependent on them to teach you; but what they are, whatever they do, becomes a means to add to your spirit development. You remain at your nadir, always ready to realize something more. You're independent of them. You're only responsible for maintaining your spirit and letting that ground-zero centering point provide renewing awareness.

Once I said this, my attention shifted. A circle with the word *helper* inscribed within it suddenly appeared in my mind, and just as suddenly it disappeared. It struck me that the apparition represented the end of my involvement with Paula as spirit therapist.

Paula handed me a note at the onset of our next meeting.

When I stood up to leave last time, my spirit flow was startled to see you change from a magnetically charged entity to a worn-out, exhausted soul. A warmth welled up in my spirit space. My empathy grew, and I felt like reaching for your hand. Then I became ambivalent. My vehicle wanted to kiss your cheek because it felt guilty for causing you pain. I centered myself in my spirit space once again. As soon as I did, I felt calmer, knowing that you didn't need an embrace. You seemed to say that you were glad you could be of help to me but that your spirit and your vehicle wished that my vehicle would not demand so much. The dominant flow I saw then was an intense concern on your part that I perhaps wouldn't have to endure as much suffering from this time on. I sensed your strength and didn't worry about you for fear that you would collapse. I could see the rejuvenative powers of your spirit flowing back, taking care of your needs.

Taking care of my spirit needs was indeed what my struggle was about. I was turning a corner in my commitment to Paula. There was a need to transfer the responsibility for actualizing her spirit life directly to her. If she was to make provisions for the continued release of her spirit, she was confronted with maintaining a posture of surveillance to ensure that she served her spirit-self rather than an intransigent vehicle. She became alarmed when I discussed this.

I'd feel terrified if you weren't here, if I didn't have someone to relate to like this.

This statement only reinforced my decision to sever this dependency. She had acquired the tools to make a spirit-centered life possible for herself. Removing myself from the helper role would compel her to establish a dependency on spirit formlessness rather than on personal-me.

Spending time alone to expand her spirit life was necessary if she was to become a spirit helper to herself. I encouraged her to place herself on a daily regimen of spirit involvement. I had already suggested ways to do this, but she was averse to practice that required self-discipline. Despite this, she began to toy with possible alternatives.

> I thought of taking a day off from work to do more for my spirit flow—feed it for awhile. It's like the urge I had recently. I wanted to park the car while driving here and walk in the fields. I could visualize myself tramping through the lovely meadows, soaking up the spirit. The idea of taking time off for spirit-me seemed more real. However, except for such fleeting feelings, I invariably get the cold-water treatment from the vehicle, which says, No! No! This isn't the right time to take a day off! I suppose I'm still relying on the forms the vehicle decides I have to live by, even though I have these intermittent phases of spirit flow that sweep over me.

> *What have you noticed about these intermittent phases?*

> It isn't the same kind of feeling it was four months ago, the first time I experienced the spirit. It has a different texture, a headier scent, fuller bodied. I can't pin it down, as you know. But it doesn't have the quick impact it did then. It's more like an old friend rather than a sudden charge. I'm also

less concerned about the ways the spirit reveals and defines itself as it fills up the crevices of my body. I used to worry if I didn't get the same reaction each time the spirit took over. I considered I wasn't doing well enough if I didn't get a tremendous differential sensation as a result of the spirit force opening up within me. I'm less concerned about getting a peak trip from it each time. I'm more accepting that it's in flux like everything else.

When I saw Paula the following week it was clear that the transfer of personal responsibility for spirit care had begun to have its effect.

I took a day off from work. I stayed in bed until late in the morning. I'd find the vehicle trying to push me out of my spirit flow, and I'd catch it right at the start with, No you don't. I was able to stay with the spirit for the entire day. It was beautiful. I went from one activity to another like a butterfly—just having a ball. It really filled me up and spilled over. It was like a pervasive flow, like the tide coming in. And it was great.

You were able to experience it rather decisively?

Yes! I'd feel it ebbing out a little, like a backwash from a wave. Then I'd take another deep breath and suck it all in again. Occasionally, I'd catch myself if I found I was rushing from one thing to another and ask, Hey! Who's doing this? Is it the spirit or the vehicle? I'd soak that spirit flow up again, and then

I'd know where I was once more. I would go on with, OK! It feels right; you're where you should be. I questioned my actions all day long, taking readings on where I was with myself and what was happening with regard to the spirit and the vehicle. I wanted to sketch early in the morning. My spirit plane said it would come, Just take it easy. So I stayed in bed awhile longer centering myself in my spirit flow and breathing my whole day's freedom more deeply. I did a lot of housework from the formless space, stopping in the middle of projects to feel what would be next. I ate, danced, wrapped packages, vacuumed, shopped, browsed in an art store and finally drove out in the rain to do some sketching. I found an interesting place and let the impressions form on the paper. I didn't feel uptight when all of the details were not exactly to scale. This is a change for me, inasmuch as I would previously have demanded that kind of perfection from myself.

Over the ensuing weeks there was a sharp increase in Paula's physical complaints—from diarrhea to extreme disruption of her menstrual cycle. In compartmentalizing her energies she had left herself vulnerable to the force of the spirit, intent on sweeping away all vehicular partitioning. I waited quietly as she campaigned for greater inner stability.

I've gone through even more physical stress than ever since I saw you. It's been very oppressive. I've had stomach cramps, a rigidity in my spine, a tightening in my right shoulder, in my thighs and neck. I had to make a very concentrated effort to center myself in the spirit flow or else I'd have a return of those physical symptoms. If I didn't structure a specific centering time, I'd be beset. I couldn't go more than three or four hours without checking in, otherwise I'd feel the binding building up again. I could sense how my vehicle was ready to club me over the head with its pressures. I think it's all tied up with a grinding of the gears of change. In addition, my period has been crazy. When I started to get those shooting pains and cramps in my abdomen, I thought I might be pregnant, so I saw my gynecologist. When he said No, I thought I'd feel a great relief. But there was none of that.

I had a flash of sensing how, as a mother, I could have been happy with the baby needing me, comfortable about the baby crying. I always hated to hear babies cry. After the baby was born, I'd tell myself that she needed me, that I should be the dutiful mother and be there for her. But it was all intellectual, my head telling me how I should be. The truth was that I was tremendously threatened by her bellowing, very put out by her demands for my attention, annoyed when she was wet or hungry. But with this new set of feelings, it was different. I realized I didn't have to feel guilty if I didn't rush to her right then and there. I could conceive of the spirit flow moving back and forth between mother and daughter, that this was the essence of the nurturing to be given an infant—not merely food. I could imagine how signals could be worked out between mother and child that would settle the baby down. Although help might not come that second, the spirit flow was perennially there. I could see how a mother could have her own spirit life too, and that mother and child could feel close, with the spirit strength making all that possible.

Paula's progress encouraged me to go further in disengaging myself. I again emphasized the need for solitary, quiet contemplation, free from distraction, so she could take more responsibility for her spirit. When Ron planned a visit to his folks, Paula used the opportunity to spend the weekend at home by herself. Her physical indisposition provided a reasonable excuse for not joining him.

It was a weird experience to spend the entire weekend with my spirit and vehicle and not be involved with much else. I found myself slipping into my spirit space to look at my form. I went through a series of episodes all weekend, in and out of the vehicular and spirit spaces. It was an experience in which the vehicle gave up the ghost. It was like trying to suppress diarrhea I couldn't. It was very painful at times. I could hear the vehicle talking to the spirit. The vehicle was saying, You've had the upper hand lately. I need a chance to be heard, too. Every so often there was a reservoir of tears that built up within the vehicular space. I could stuff it down for so long, and then it popped out. So I let the tears flow. I was telling the vehicle, OK, you've had your say, now we can go back to the free-flowing spirit again. It isn't going to solve anything, or make it better in the long run, to keep crying. But if it makes you feel better for the moment, then go ahead and cry.

So I went through this thing about crying, not crying. I could hear myself talking to my vehicle again: You want to suffer? Go ahead and suffer. You don't have to, you know. All I could do, without the spirit space available, was to concentrate every bit of energy on avoiding the pain and hurt, soothing old wounds. It was clearer that in programming my life I had been taken over by my vehicle and then reduced to exhaustion. I found out, however, that I could not stay completely in the spirit consciousness and block everything else out. The vehicle was too strong.

As the weekend wore on, more of me was able to remain in the spirit space and look at the pain, and feel the pain at the same time. I couldn't pretend about the suffering anymore, but had to live through it. And I couldn't stop crying. It was out of my hands, out of my control. As I cried, I realized I was not crushed by its effects. It was quite a situation. I talked to friends. I went through more painful episodes. I turned to dancing by myself, feeling the spirit space, using the physical movement of the dance to let the pain dissolve, trying new techniques drawn from the spirit flow to overcome it. I used my hands and my spirit in the dance movements to figuratively remove piece after piece of the vehicle. It was a real encounter of feeling the physical structuredness of the vehicle, then letting the spirit force go deeper and deeper into the symbolic removal of the pieces of the form—grabbing them, ripping and tearing out the vehicle's holds on my body.

Finally, I found great strength in talking it out, feeling it out. Then periods of exhaustion followed. I went back and forth this way and by Sunday things had changed. I felt happy, so relieved. The parable in the Bible, Why beholdest thou the mote that is in thy brother's eye, but considerest not the beam that is in thine own eye, hit me like a ton of bricks. Here I was scrambling around, figuring that I was such a goodie-goodie, that I was so aware of things, supposedly. If I was so perfectly put together, such a perfect person, how come I was still struggling with my personal problems? I realized that the more I thought of achieving and accomplishing, the more nasty I would be to others who, supposedly, weren't doing as well as I thought they should. I had to stop and consider the beam in my eye. I had to be responsible for me, the essence-me, so I could be a better person. I went back to the things I was taught in church—that people are not strong enough, in and of themselves, to handle the burdens of the world. I could see where I might love people, love to help out, but I didn't have the strength, the wisdom, or the wherewithal to take on their burdens with my vehicular-self. I would only tear myself down trying to do the impossible. Finally, using the dance movement as an expression of my spirit-self, I gathered all of the pieces and fragments of the vehicle together and said, Take it, I can't handle it. I gave it up, not from despair, resignation or bitterness, but I gave it up to the one who is supposed to be there—to God. I had never been able to do that in my entire life. I'd wanted to. I'd felt the need to do it, the desire, the hunger to surrender to Him. But suddenly I was there. It was like swinging off a chandelier; it was so good. That spiritual space in the trunk of my body has stayed with me ever since. The pushing out of the vehicle opened up different planes of consciousness. Sometimes the boundaries of the spirit space disappeared as if they didn't exist anymore as boundaries. From that point on the spirit was no longer a completely defined entity coming in and out of a shadowy form. It went into an osmotic flow. It broke the bounds of thinking about it. I could see myself as a centipede with all those feet. It went beyond being able to distinguish placing one foot in front of another in moving about. It became much more total.

I find that because of that intense experience I merely have to give myself a couple of cue words, cue feelings, cue physical exercises, or cue anything to get into the spirit space. It's almost as if I can do something else while the spirit flow is going on at another level. I find myself fixing meals and drawing on the spirit space at the same time, using anything and everything around me to bring my essence flow into it. When the spirit force slipped away, I knew it wasn't going to disappear forever. That was one thing I would get panicky about. The vehicle would say, See! It's not working so you better not depend on it that much! But the spirit plane was really good to me not only on that weekend but ever since. I feel much more comfortable with this power. It's a happy thing, and it's great to take it matter-of-factly. Ever since that experience I sense a greater enjoyment of everything. I feel more like the real me. Things just flow. When I'm that spirit-me, I don't worry about getting things done. I just feel comfortable doing the things I enjoy doing. I sense I'm firmer in my body. I look better to me and am a lot happier for it. This is happening even though I haven't used the spirit force to structure a lesson plan at home.

Whatever relief I felt concerning Paula's ability to use that ingoing, solitary process to deepen her spirit reserve was tempered by another outbreak of unhappiness.

I can't live day by day in the spirit space and not try, after functioning beautifully that way, to make the spirit flow between Ron and me. If I have this spirit force within me, I want to give it to other people. I want them to know this, too.

Paula never thought twice about making the spirit flow between Ron and her. The purity of her spirit life had again been infiltrated by a resurgent vehicular force determined to impose new conditions on Ron. It was foolhardy for me to intervene. So I maintained my usual position of watchful waiting.

For several weeks Paula was unwavering.

> When I try to engage him in the spirit flow, he gets rattled. He feels the rug is being pulled out from under him. He doesn't know where he is with me. He's so terrified and repulsed by the spirit process. He told me that he thought he knew himself pretty well. But he's so threatened by my spirit flow.

Paula's failure to instigate spirit rapport with Ron was matched by a fading enthusiasm in her affair. Her encounters with Brandon had become more direct and she was seeing through the illusions of their relationship, beyond the sexual intimacies of earlier contacts. The resulting awareness provided Paula with more understanding of Brandon's personal foibles.

> In the beginning I wanted to know him more. But as our relationship continued, I had to know me more. I've been drawing on spirit strength within me instead of setting it aside in deference to him. For awhile I felt sucked into his game. I have a funny feeling about him now. He doesn't always have the courage of his convictions. I was very angry at him recently. I felt he enjoyed making other people feel small so that he could create an image of importance. What has bothered me is that he seems to derive a great deal of satisfaction from this. I haven't been an angel, but I'm very uncomfortable when my vehicle has an impulse of lording it over others that way. I realize that the sex thing was something I needed from him in

order to bolster myself—like nourishment from an emergency can of rations, a way of keeping my body from crumbling as a result of a deficiency of inner strength. But I'm finding a different strength now. I don't need to keep my body running to a motel room with him in order to provide the nutrients through sex. I don't need to rush to him to be completed. That's just another vehicular trip—the idea that if only I get together with him then everything else is going to be great.

Things were moving fast, bringing Paula to a push-and-pull of vehicular and spirit forces.

My spirit is grieving. I know now that Ron doesn't enjoy relating on a deep level. It makes me feel very empty, stale, incomplete and defeated to live with someone who lacks that ability and desire. He obviously can't grow. Should I worry about the future? Must I have someone with like interests to share? How much can I stand living with a rigid person? Would I be better off being by myself? Do I have a right to expect anything from anybody else? I keep having a recurring feeling, despite all that's happened, that I should hang on to the marriage. Ron's a kind person. If I want him to accept me, shouldn't I start accepting him first? I could really make it hard for myself, being single and struggling with a bunch of bills. It's nice not to have to worry about that.

I hear my vehicle giving support to this by saying, Why flog yourself? You've got a secure haven with him. Take it easy, sock a few more dollars in the savings account, plan your summer activities.

But those feelings don't last very long before something else begins to churn within me—questions like, Why did I marry him? Is it a cross I've got to bear?

Then the vehicle steps in again: You know the facts. You can get a divorce in two or three days if he agrees to it. You can run down to Haiti, and it will all be over.

Then another part chimes in: That's too easy. You should make the marriage work; show society that you learned your lesson from the first marriage.

But what it comes down to is that I'm a dying person at home. If I'm spirit-me, then the marriage is over. If I leave the spirit behind, as I've done in the past, then the vehicle takes over and I'm dead too. I lose either way. Ron and I can talk about the grocery bill or about buying a new car. We can get projects done that either of us feels is essential. But there's that something that's missing between us. It's being married to someone who is incapable of growing, I suppose. That's when I start feeling the sexual needs of the body cropping up. I want something more with him, and I'd feel happy if, at least, there could be some kind of intimacy—sexual or spirit.

Yet no matter what I try my spirit-self laughs at me and says, There you are, gnashing your teeth, it won't do any good.

If I flow with the spirit, the vehicle growls, What did the spirit ever really do for you? Nothing!

I can go so long in either space, then everything breaks down. I'm not spirit-centered or vehicle-centered. I'm just sliding, drifting along, flying around from one set of feelings to another.

Only Paula could determine how far she was prepared to go in living a spirit life, on her path, in her way—apart from what I, or anyone else, might do. She had relied so heavily, and for so long, on vehicular autonomy that its structured patterns remained a primary source of security for her. I remembered what she once had said, with a certain testiness:

I know that my vehicle has believed in its omnipotent powers, that if it tries hard enough, it can beat anybody's system, that one way or another it can get the other person to give in. Stick it out, and eventually people are going to get tired of fighting you. Then you're there and you've won.

In the ensuing showdown, Paula's vehicle whiplashed her unmercifully. Whether Paula would help herself further would hinge on her freeing herself from a dependency on marriage as a form. Although she'd remarked on a number of occasions that she couldn't bear the failure of a second marriage, my distinct impression was that she was really afraid to be in the world without someone being there for her in a personal, subject-object way.

The marriage was really secondary to the main issue,

which was whether she wanted more of a spirit-self. If she did fulfill that, she would begin to flow more harmoniously with the whole of life, experiencing no rejection or denigration of Ron. She would simply see him as being at a certain, limited place on his developmental journey. If she was more of spirit, she would find it easier to live with him, even though they might have less in common. She might even leave him at some point, but it would not be because she considered him intolerable. It would be because she had learned that her life required more spirit involvement than he was able to live out for himself or with her. In that sense, her concern and affection for him could continue even though she recognized a spirit differential deserving of honest acceptance.

Whatever I had learned had come from my own transpersonal awakening. Paula had her own dragon to slay. When her sulking and cynicism persisted, I described certain attempts at self-help on my own path. I explained in detail how I had used a period of practice, alone, to deal with a sliver of vehicular stress that very morning. As I did so, I knew that the umbilical cord between us had been severed.

A few days before seeing Paula again, my spirit presented me with a startling decree: I was to stop seeing her. It was not clear whether it would be temporary or permanent. The idea of cutting off all contact, in the midst of her full-blown low, seemed almost cruel. What if such a decision was unwarranted or premature? Could I really trust my spirit to that extent? Could she rely on her tenuous spirit capacities that much? I was faced with more and more questions, yet with only one course to follow.

Paula was not her usual self when she arrived for what was to be our last session. A serious and deliberate attitude had replaced her casualness.

> What you said to me last time was just like a shot in the arm. It got me right back on the track. I wrote to my mother last week and told her that my digging into myself was a way of shedding my anguish, that plugging into something bigger—the spirit source—was a means for me to really help myself.
> She wrote back and said, Great! I'm sure it will work out if you don't try to force things, if you allow them to happen more.
> I told her some of the things we've been talking about. She said she was so happy for me. It sounded as if she valued my understanding of me for myself.

> *What did we share that you're referring to?*

> Basically, the fact that I'll have rough times, and that's to be expected. A lot of people think that by attending church, by following the trappings of their religion, being pious and saying their prayers, they should be spared from having troubles. It ain't so. I've come to realize that trouble is going

to be there regardless. Also, I need to become a servant to the spirit, not to boast or make a big thing of what I'm able to do. The more I think and say Me! Me! Me! the more difficult I'm going to make it for myself. I'll never know when I'm going to get egg on my face. If I keep my attention on strengthening the spirit, I won't be concerned with who's first or best.

I gather there's something about suffering, as we talked about it last time, that you've been mulling over.

Yes. I got offshoots of your message concerning your own personal struggle. Suffering was always something to be ashamed of for me. Anything negative about myself was taboo. So I never revealed my inner pain, sorrow, hatred, envy. Hogwash! If those emotions are there, if they're incapacitating, I should be able to talk with someone who won't be offended by them. I don't have to avoid subjects because they're unpleasant. That's the coward's way, the easy way.

When you spoke of the journey on your path, in your desire to know more, to help yourself, the ways you've practiced to move things along, it was a tremendous comfort. Someone else might have been bothered by your description of struggling. But you put your finger on something that upset me as a child—people would say that the more I came to know, the more I would realize how little I really knew. That idea left me feeling crushed. If I struggled to know, I'd still end up feeling inadequate. That meant I'd never have enough answers. I realize now, in getting to know and discover things for myself, that all kinds of horizons can open up. It's like an onion, the more layers I peel off the more of the core can open up. There's no worry about the future or concern about the past on that path, no judgment to be made. It's a way of accepting myself at that point in time, and validation of all the things I've wanted to believe in. Pieces of the jigsaw that have been bugging me, that I couldn't reconcile, have fallen into place. If I look at some of the threatening problems I've been experiencing—with this knowledge of being on the path —I feel less fear of them. They lose their hold on me, particularly if I show them to you—one who is not afraid of them and has been through that kind of agony, too.

You mean the segment of a vehicular form which has no basis in reality—the illusion.

Right! The illusions can be removed with the cleanness and thoroughness of a surgeon's scalpel. When I can focus on a fantasy and center the power of spirit strength on it, it's like a large magnet pulling out all the vehicular debris. This makes the suffering worth experiencing now. It isn't a giant octopus inking up the water all around me, or a nameless terror. It means that any kind of suffering I encounter can be dealt with very expertly. I don't even have to have a special talent for that. I plug into the spirit plane and the talent is there. Whatever I need is there in that flow and space.

You've been trying to explain this to your mother, I assume.

In my letter I explained how I had viewed marriage in relation to certain programs. With Brig I had tried to set it up in one way. After I left the hospital, I worked out another set of combinations, and with Ron it was different series of arrangements. When a problem presented itself in one area, like sex, I would think this, that, and the other thing. I'd set up something else in trying to overcome my discouragement. It began to dawn on me lately that approaching all this in a rational, logical, and factual way was getting me nowhere. Now a whole new way of looking at my life has opened up through the spirit plane. So my mother was delighted when I explained to her that I wasn't handling my situation from that analytic, psychological collection of conceptions.

You were sharing the newer ways you're viewing the marital form.

Yes, but mainly viewing myself on an entirely new plane. The basic thing was not to be stuck on a trip of hating myself. I needed to be free of the notion of inadequacy or worthlessness as a result of not being able to accomplish all the things the vehicle had set for me to do with regard to marriage. If Ron liked a particular type of food, I'd strive to please him by making that dish so he'd appreciate me more—while all the time I was seething inside because the marriage wasn't really working in the first place. My way of living has been to deny all this. Some women may be able to spend their whole lives pretending in the way I have. If that's their bag, and they have no need to go beyond, that's fine for them. I can't. There are too many things I need to enjoy to sacrifice myself for a set of fantasies.

I gather you're saying that if you view yourself in the identity of the vehicle, then you must be successful in the different phases of your life in accordance with its preconceived judgments.

Right. And when it does that, it encapsulates my entire spirit flow and brings me to the point of cracking up. I'm only now beginning to realize that my mother and I have a lot in common with regard to vehicular problems.

You seem to be reaching out to your mother, offering her your spirit flow.

This has been true of the whole time I've seen you. She's been afraid that I'd get so tied down with analyzing that I'd waste my life picking things apart.

Perhaps fearful of your analyzing and picking her apart.

And afraid that I'd call her less-than-perfect and expect her to change her life. I don't expect her to change or tear her hair out as an act of penitence. In my writing to her, I was just looking at things like a child with a new toy, seeing all the pieces and being fascinated by their different relationships. As I told her, everything I feel and think generates some sort of electrical energy which takes up space. I can't see the air I breathe, but it takes up space, and I must deal with it. The same is true of my emotions, my thoughts and my physical movements. I told her that in growing up I had to deny and submerge my feelings. When I did this, it took more and more energy and conscious effort to keep the feelings hidden and controlled. There wasn't much left of my flow to use in work, to attempt a new project, or whatever else I might have felt important to realize. It impoverished me. It was like being sick with the flu continually. The loss of the spirit was a terrible thing because it cheated me. I was like a person with emphysema. I couldn't breathe. I couldn't work. I had all that pollution in my lungs and in my soul, asphyxiated by my pain, by my negative thoughts, the hatreds and fears. My letter was really a way of sharing with her the way I had fallen on my face as a result of my rigidity in dealing with things. I wasn't pointing a finger of blame anywhere. I wasn't preaching, merely telling her that's the way it was. I was describing the understanding coming from the spirit. I just had to share that nice, good, healthy, comfortable, delightful awakening with her.

She, in turn, picked up the fact that I wasn't saying, Now that I'm so happy, let me pass these great things on to you, or You must do this because I want you to be happy in the same way. That would have put pressure on her that I didn't want to exert. But her letter, in answer to mine, was the most enthusiastic I've received in my entire life.

I sense your mother might have felt, Thank God it's

working out for her, as a result of her deep concern for you.

I can see her heaving a big sigh of relief about the daughter with the problem, and feeling freer to attend to matters that are personal and important to her. It's been a kind of cross for her to bear.

How do you feel about finding yourself on the threshhold of a different relationship with her, leaving the status of being her child?

It's a feeling of coming home. The energy can make a complete turn and renew itself instead of leaking out and getting lost somewhere. My saying the unspoken things lately, instead of keeping up the fantasy life with her, has given her more freedom to respond within her own capacities. I sense there are things she's not yet able to handle, so I find myself giving her a thought or idea to mull over.

That tends to put you in a more responsible position with her. How do you feel about that?

Good. It feels the way it should—natural to me.

But when you leave home and go into the spirit flow, you're leaving the nest, the form, the secular syndrome of the family.

Which used to frighten me—her threat to send me away to an orphanage. But now if I admit I've been born as form, and then I go to the spirit release, it's a feeling of Hurrah! It's as natural as breathing, the sense of being at home in the universe. It's like a kid walking out of the house and into the world outside, with no thought about what's proper or improper, just enjoying what is. There's been an awful vehicular crunch for me these last few weeks, as you know. It was another lesson with regard to personal responsibility, the fact that I've got to take care of me. The vehicle made responsibility out to be a terrible monster. It kept me forever distraught; any letdown on my part and I'd be done in. The feeling was so horrendous I had to run away from acknowledging what I felt. I created all kinds of subterfuges to avoid facing the responsibility of feeling me.

What we've been talking about bears on you and me, too. What do you sense about your relationship with me now?

Your spirit flow has been a big help to me, but I see less of a helper role for you as it's evolved.

How do you feel about that?

It's great that it's happening. Right now it feels as if it was never any other way but the way it is now. I don't want to ever forget the way it was. It's easy to fall back into the vehicular trap.

I think you'll find the very nature of the spirit process produces change. It has its own power to do that. There have been various changes for me, as there have been for you, since I started seeing you.

I recognize that the process has changed things for you too. I remember any number of times you felt differences in the ways you were viewing me—how you felt me emerging, the little insights that came from your spirit plane—pop, pop, pop. When someone is tormented, as I've been, it isn't fun for you. That's when it's grim. You'd sense my pain—but you wouldn't be trapped in my suffering, hurting as I'd be hurting. You'd be free, maintaining a certain peacefulness within yourself, despite what I'd be feeling.

If you are essentially vehicular, then the responsibility falls very heavily on me to be that much more spirit centered in order to be a stable spirit rudder for both of us.

Put it this way. If you have to constantly take care of me, you're going to be drained. You've got to spend more time in your own spirit space. That's the only way life will be fun for you, the delight that you've referred to as arising out of the spirit source—the gaiety and playfulness beyond having a dismal shadow following you.

Let me define a bit more, and share with you what I sense I've gone through. Most of what has happened has been choiceless for me. My spirit force has decided the ways I should relate to you. I've simply served it beyond my individuality as a separate person. At various stages it has said, This is what makes sense, this is what has to be done.
Now it's saying that I am no longer responsible for you,

a parent looking after you, protecting you from vehicular suffering. It is telling me that from now on you are responsible for your strife, any personal neglect on your part is your problem. It is taking me out of any remaining obligation for the way you might give yourself hurt, or even the way you help yourself with that pain. It only feels a remaining interest in relating to you, spirit-to-spirit. It is convinced that, since you've established a footing in the essence of spirit, you'll be able to function that way and build on it in the future.

So now my spirit is saying that you take care of you. You're on your path. If you want to share your journey with me at a later time, that's a point of meeting. We can then compare notes and realizations of the spirit process.

I've been feeling in the full flow of the spirit. But when you tell me this, it chops it off completely. I can feel myself clutching, no longer moving with the spirit.

I just explained what my spirit is saying.

But I hear you telling me to sink or swim.

No! It's more like—a day or two after a patient has been operated on, the doctor makes the rounds and says to the patient, It's time to get out of bed. The patient says, Get out of bed? I can't, it hurts too much. But there's no choice. Sure it's going to hurt, but then as the patient starts to flex his muscles, he realizes that it was helpful for him to leave that cozy protection after all. My spirit plane is saying that it knows you can do this.

You know I can do it. I know I can do it. But I saw a vehicular trap ahead of me when you said, No longer. I could get stuck on that vehicular plane again, very much like a kid who regresses when the new baby comes home from the hospital and he starts wetting his pants again or sucking his thumb. There's a time and place for everything.

Your vehicle is trying to keep the home fires burning. My spirit says it is one hundred percent free of what was. I hear your vehicle saying, Make it ninety-nine percent, so that I'll have a chance to have what I've had.

I know me. There are times when I may agonize.

My spirit says that I am through taking care of you, and I obey. I have no choice. My spirit is done with my being responsible for feeding you enough spirit to keep you going. I don't feel you need that anymore. Secondly, my spirit is saying that if you get into trouble, and it feels like the end of the world, your spirit capacity will be available to take care of you. You don't need any form, including me, to do that. If my spirit holds out one percent— which it isn't—then I'm compromising it. I'm not about to downgrade that awareness—that you can provide for yourself, even under the worst kinds of distress, through your own spirit power.

I'm feeling some tension, but I can accept that.

Even if you can't accept it, my spirit is saying that's all right too.

I was really asking you to define more fully the process of continuous change. But to say, Nevermore—

My spirit is saying that nevermore will it view you in the way it has in the past—as needing to depend on me in those ways.

I understand. You're looking at it from two different planes. I've been experiencing something new these last few days too. But everybody can use a little help at a certain point. There will still be times in my life when I'll be down—not out, but down.

That presents a critical point. Let's suppose that you're down, and you're ready to scream for help because you can't stop going down. Let's assume that I still represent to you the symbol which saves you. You'll forever be looking to me to be saved.

Looking to you and being stuck.

Looking for that one form which you believe you still need. That will never permit you to really be free. The important question confronting my spirit-self at this point involves the matter of freedom. How do we move beyond where we've been so that you become even freer—not only less dependent on form, but freer to be with it all. You can't possibly have a real spirit flow in a relationship with another human being—man, woman, anybody—unless you're free of that last, tiny vehicular fragment which wants to hold back, hold out, and hold on.

I see.

What do you see?

I'm laughing because I see that your point is well taken. That's the fantasy point. When does the child become a woman? She crosses over when she sees that last fantasy she's had as a child exploded. It's the vehicle still trying to circumvent, still seeing her as a child. If I'm an integrated person, I see the vehicle as a child. That just came to me.

I see mine as an infant, a newborn infant who demands omnipotence. It's got to control it all because it feels so helpless, so desperate in its attempt to cope with the confusion. If I try to serve that infant—even a fraction—it puts me back in a bind again because the infant wants to grab, to clench, to make sure, to force things into its conceptions. By doing that I alienate myself from my spirit flow and its potential for regeneration of my spirit-self.

I haven't been able to go back that far, but I can sense now that if I am in the spirit flow and living it, then I'm into an adulthood which is not an end in itself but a place where many people hope to live.

That's being one with the spirit autonomy where the harmony of it all is the guiding light—the antithesis of infantile striving for autonomy which comes from the fantasy you spoke of. That's why daily practice becomes important as a way of maintaining a connectedness with spirit omniscience. Relying on that spirit force will clear out the fallacious distortions and thereby allow the body to become filled with light.

I sense for myself how the vehicle still tries to make logic through words and other thought symbols.

By doing that, it keeps raping your experiential spirit flow.

Ron said a couple of nights ago that sex was a reward. He told me that he could relax and enjoy making love only when everything else was in order, like the house having been cleaned up beforehand. I didn't get mad or rip into him when he told me this. All I felt was, Gee! That's the illusion of making things just right! Under the circumstances, I become a kind of prostitute. Instead of being paid with money, I'm rewarded when I fulfill his expectations of living by his programs.

He's simply at his own point of reference on his evolutionary trail.

Knowing that has helped me to see things more clearly with him. I realize that pushing Ron to get with it has been a way of throwing stones at him. I had the idea that he had the problem, he should be on the chopping block. He had to suffer, too. It was as if I had to make him squirm for what Brig had done to me. I said to myself, Whoops! That would really be a bad trip.

The way it is now, I don't expect to solve my life at any one instant. I'm satisfied to feel things as they come, letting them jell and fall into place. I don't expect to learn everything and have all the answers. I'm very comfortable in this process of becoming. It's what I've wanted all these years.

That brings me back to my spirit-self in relation to your acceptance of change.

You're certainly harping on that, aren't you?

I need to know. But I don't have to know this minute.

You've mentioned it four or five times.

Only because we haven't settled it.

I like the idea of your spirit growing, too. This past week I've been doing the kinds of daily practice you've emphasized. When the vehicle said, You don't need that stuff, I've been able to ignore its catcalls. When I think of the last few weeks, and how depressed I was, the idea of maintaining a practice regimen has begun to hit home. I've felt better as I've taken time out to quietly feel. I sense how essential and natural this is as I look back at that black period when I didn't involve myself in daily practice.

Up to now, you've tended to wait until you were on the edge of disaster before giving attention to your flow and to what was going on within you.

That's true. But these last weeks have represented the last throes of cliffhanging. It's part of having lived in a world of pipe dreams and false hopes. As a kid, I daydreamed; I wrote poetry. I idealized everything in order to avoid experiencing what was true. I'm sure I can avoid those unreal trips if I check myself each day. I'd have a reference point that would keep me centered properly. It's something I not only want to do but need to do. Apparently I had to go through that black hole these past few weeks. It frightened the devil out of me. I was furious and acted like a little brat. I was stomping around, throwing things, having one big temper tantrum. But it was something I seemed to have to live out. To see it the way I did helped me understand what I was doing.

I believe it would help you if you didn't see me for a period of time. I'm not saying how long. It would be an opportunity for you to try your wings, to see what it's like to work with yourself.

It's something I hadn't thought about when I came today. I viewed myself more independently since seeing the light in that black hole. Now that I've verbalized some of these things out loud, I can hear part of me saying, Ouch! Maybe I went too far in admitting and confessing it all.

Do you want to take back anything you've said?

No! The vehicle doesn't like the idea, but spirit-me feels very comfortable about it.

I'm trying to explore this so that I'm not being arbitrary about when I should see you again.

Right now I can feel the vehicle trying to take over while the spirit is saying, Cut it out. From the spirit space, the idea of not seeing you for awhile is re-freshingly pleasant. Taking a sabbatical to put things into daily practice is a hopeful prospect. But the vehicle is rebelling within me. It's annoyed and say-ing, Aha! You're really doing it to me, aren't you? You're finally forcing me to be responsible. I'm no longer that important to you. The vehicle is clutching for all it's worth. It's really funny, seeing it skidding around like that. I can't help giggling as I'm watching it go through its sad sack routine.

Paula's giggling was so infectious that we were re-duced to uncontrollable laughter. There was a fluttering and choking in her voice as she tried to speak, but it was no use. Every time she attempted to say something, it only brought us to the brink of side-splitting hysterics. We were only able to gesture to one another. I was the first to speak after we regained our composure.

Sort of like your vehicle is saying, You don't really like me, do you? If you loved me, you could never do this to me.

Right! It's putting on a big act. But that tells me that it's all right to go ahead.

Suppose we left it formless as to when we see each other again. That would be a spirit way of handling it.

As Paula slowly closed the door behind her, an empti-ness descended, pervading the room and my person as well. Somehow it was all right.

Although I had evolved in the work, and apparently Paula had gained from the spirit process, there was a growing disparity between what I sensed was possible in spirit help and the results so far. One important clue was having to perform new feats, or so I felt; having to add to the repertoire of devices each week to move the work along.

As long as I remained the implied source for providing help in terms of these props, I was attached to the role of the authority. I had needed these tools in the past in order to spare myself from having to face personal insecurity. Since I was new at this, the devices were a kind of insurance in protecting the patient as well as myself from my limitations.

However, just as the drum had been a valuable bridge for me, it also was a throwaway. I could look back and see quite clearly that techniques had kept the person in the other chair at a safe distance: the tools had been helpful, but they restricted the relationship. I was outgrowing this tidy way of working, and I felt that the patients would welcome something more.

I still had a problem identifying what could be done to deepen and extend the feeling process. If I tossed aside the gimmicks, all that would remain would be the other person and myself, with nothing to stand in the way of a total spirit encounter.

The spirit posited a type of involvement which was at the expense of all my professionalism. It wasn't that I felt particularly faithful to my clinical mystique, but the image had served as a buffer from intrusions by patients who would want to get too personal, and spared me from the disquieting idea of going all-out, dissolving into transpersonal union with them.

The spirit within me was better prepared for this than my structured-self, so we struck a bargain. I would approach with caution, feeling my way, using moderation—a kind of middle ground. Whatever energies were set in motion would have to dovetail into that plan. Any action would deal with bindings restricting direct release.

To dissolve my circumscribed approach in favor of one-pointed experiencing meant giving myself over to raw power, and possibly direct penetration into another's being. Again, I had to trust my spirit even further. My training was to draw a person out, not invade his domain with power my professional-self could not control. But essence told me it was possible to retain a spirit base within me while entering another's deepest levels.

When one is really ready, opportunity knocks. A year had passed since I had seen Lynn. I hadn't been aware of her progress until she called and came to see me. Even though she wasn't applying herself fully in practice sessions, she was making some effort, which I had not anticipated. A spirit process was going on. As I look back on that session, I recognize that she came to see me in order to free herself from being on the fence.

I didn't think I could do what I did with you last time, as easily as I was able to. I liked the feeling I got from that last session. It's as if life has become less of an effort as a result. I don't give a darn about a lot of things now I used to worry about. I probably couldn't have known this unless I had grown to a certain extent, and the experience with you last time underscored that. The direction we took was right, like I was at a certain point which confirmed something for me.

Before, I would worry about what people would think of me. The experience last time seemed to remove a lot of the thinking about judging and being judged. A lot of that has left me, but not all of it. The judging still haunts me to a degree. But I seem to be able to do things now or say things that I was afraid to before, like extending or asserting myself. I know people are making judgments, but it doesn't bother me that much now.

When I'm by myself I feel better, happier, lighter. I've felt stimulated, excited in the past by certain things. I don't know whether that stimulation has been a hoax. What I'm saying is I don't know whether the good feelings are real or whether it's just another trick. So even though I feel the happiness I felt in that space with you when there was nothing I had to do to make things happen, I still don't trust the flow that much. It's like I still can't believe it's true.

Even though the flow feels right, it seems to take me away from the ordinary, normal life I've known. It estranges me from certain people, and I haven't found anyone who understands this or who's on the same track. It's as if I have to go all the way with this now. Yet I feel I'm on the fence. I can't live the way I have in the past, or with certain people, and yet I'm not ready to chuck it all, either.

Nothing consequential resulted from Lynn's session, and that left things up in the air. She called me afterwards, and I sensed even more of this disquiet within her. She complained that she was still unable to experience with any other person what she had lived out with me, although she admitted she had been able to reproduce that flow for herself at times. A few times she mentioned Marty as someone she wished she could have it with.

Hidden within the deeper recesses of the human heart is a secret wish which all of us have had at one time or another: to find the perfect soul-mate. We each yearn to have the barren spaces in our being filled by the on-rushing delights of another's stirrings. We want to give that other the sacred and unlived essence of our very soul and, by doing so, end our woeful loneliness. Often, we consider this longing to be a sign of immaturity, a throwback to adolescent romanticism. We usually don't talk about it. Still, the desire persists. We savor our inner hope, knowing the vague image of this imagined lover, companion, confidante, is too precious to forgo.

Because she couldn't find anyone who could resonate with her on a feeling, spirit plane, Lynn felt adrift. She had been seeking that special man to give herself to, and now she was particularly isolated from the mainstream of man-woman involvements. She was still searching for her ideal in human form. She wanted her personality-self to be loved completely, unstintingly. She was stuck with a thinking ego-ideal.

If she had come back to me to be pushed over the spirit edge, I was not prepared to do it. First of all, I was not fully aware of what was possible in using untapped spirit power to make that crossing. I had a growing but still limited grasp of the spirit soul-mate process. I too had known the striving to find my counterpart in form, that unique girl or woman who would supposedly complete my being merely by her presence. But having realized the futility of that, I was prepared to yield to a longing-for beyond that search.

It was easier for me to understand this after reexamining my brief contact with the Master. Even though I was not seeing him in person, I continued to feel his presence. Whenever the soulful need rose to a heightened level, my longing for renewed contact with the Master would return. Its intensity deepened within me as a result of my increased willingness to trust its demands, and I too craved the opportunity to resonate with another soul on this pure level. When I denied myself the opportunity to return to him, it only intensified my longing-for flow. There was only one other way I could release and direct that flow: in living experience. I was drawn toward a living-for and a yearning to know oneness with a feeling ideal.

Lynn wrote to me two months later.

Dear Carl: Just a note to let you know what's been happening. My car broke down and is in need of considerable repair. As soon as it's on the road again, I'll call you. I'm anxious to get back to you. I try practicing what you taught me, sometimes with success, sometimes not. My biggest difficulty is disciplining myself to make the time to practice. I almost always benefit from the results.

I have decided to marry Marty. The ceremony will be next month. I simply closed my eyes and threw a dart at the calendar. My feeling is that if I'm ever to remarry, it might as well be now. Marty and I struggle and fight a lot, but with it all, I really dig the guy. He's a good person, affectionate, considerate—qualities I like in a man. I'm having some difficulty thinking about someone other than myself, but even that is smoothing out. In fact, it's kind of nice to care for someone. I hope I'll see you reasonably soon. Love, Lynn.

A few months passed between her note and our next meeting. In that time, our matched needs were building to a crescendo. The spirit process was at work in both Lynn and me. A certain interpenetration had been effected—not me with her, but essence with essence, soul with soul. The flow had its own life and was taking its course. The work was working.

Previously I might have thought there was a difference in our searching, but I knew now we were both seeking the same Beloved. I began to sense a possible crossing to infinite love—an attainable reality, as opposed to the superficial, suffering soul-mate fantasy to which she had been attached. She still didn't know she was looking for that—but I knew it. I had fewer misgivings now. So when Lynn came to see me three days after her marriage—which did seem a bit astonishing—I was fully prepared for an excursion into all levels of the soul. I had a sense of heightened anticipation, and she must have had a similar life-force building in her. She had had an appointment a day earlier, but it had snowed heavily. When she called to postpone the session, she was greatly disappointed. By the following day, we were both eager to meet.

Lynn began by reminding me of the virtues of spirit practice at home, but she gingerly excused herself from more than passing responsibility.

> I'm really not disciplined enough to sit down and do it; I can't find the time. In the morning I'm rushed before going to work. At night I have meals to prepare—that sort of thing.

I immediately decided on a different tack, choosing to split off her vehicular, personality-I from interfering with the pure feeling flow that might otherwise generate between us.

> *You have been talking about yourself, your I. Can you explain to me who that I is?*

> It's that part that takes over. It's a feeling that it's not me, because when I begin to struggle, it's like I'm reaching up—like trying to swim to the surface. It's my attempt to reach out, to get beyond the

maze I'm in, the entanglement. As soon as I can feel myself doing that I feel relieved, and the part that makes me feel restricted and attempts to suffocate me drops away. But me or somebody else has to watch that part so it doesn't creep back and get to my me again.

The me you refer to would be outside the boundaries of that part, the vehicle. You smiled when I said that just now.

Well, it's familiar; I can relate to the free me. I just enjoy hearing you say it. The sense of it touches me.

We did have an experience together, the time you were outside your personality and I was outside any personality that might have existed for me. We were both in the clear, boundless field of essence flow. As you relate to me now, what do you sense is possible for you in stepping outside your body or your personality, allowing yourself to begin experiencing a more soulful flow with me?

I'm a little tense about it, even though I want to do it. That's personality-me. I realize I'm still trying, driving and pushing myself.

The real alive me is that flow outside my body, free of that form, free of personality-me.

I know what you're saying.

You're actually experiencing separation, *and then experiencing* purity, *the feeling flow that begins to evolve as a result of that separation, then* surrendering *to that open, clear, free, soulful, natural space.*

Yes, I can sense that. It's like watching a film. Now personality-me is trying to prevent it from happening. Soulful-me gets out of its clutches, starts to drift, then it drifts to a certain point and can't move any more. Even though it's separate, personality-me keeps trying to interfere, trying to stop it.

Is there anything your free soulful-self can experience with my free soulful-self?

Not yet. I can't do it.

When you said that, I sensed an emotion of frustration present within you. Which was at work do you suppose, the personality or free you, just then?

It was a disgusted feeling. I sensed I couldn't go any further. I think it was me against me.

What does that tell you?

Apparently, it wasn't soulful-me because every time soulful me was talking I felt good. The soul knows the personality was doing the thinking.

Then when you are thinking about things, thinking about you, it's personality-you, I gather. The soul just feels that pure bliss.

Yes!

Can you allow the soulful flow within you to open up, to awaken more, to let it take over as you surrender to it more?

Personality-me says No! and the personality becomes very conscious of this room and me, my body, everything material.

See if you can continue to experience your soulful-self and its flow not really being that interested or concerned with the personality, because the feelings of bliss are so delicious that the other nonsense, the mental activity, isn't worth bothering about. It's just noise. Sort of a who-needs-that attitude.

It goes just so far.

What do you observe of that point where it stops?

Do you remember when we first did that preinduction thing: I was sitting here in the chair and you asked me to get up from the chair and move around. It felt as if off to my left side was a force or presence holding me, not wanting to let me go. Now personality-me has let me move, but for only a short distance. It keeps trying to control me at a certain point.

When that personality-you insists on running things, can you give it your soulful flow?

No, I can't do it. I can't trust personality-me getting that flow from soulful-me.

Suddenly, there was a rush of energy moving out of my body, pushing into her field.

I'm giving personality-you my soulful flow right now, whatever my soul can give to that personality-you which insists on controlling. I'm feeling a compassion for its uptightness, its fears, insecurities, the ideas it lives off about being all alone in the world, not having anybody, on and on. And so my soulful flow goes out to it.

My soulful flow doesn't seem to have that compassion. It just enjoys being free and doesn't want to pay any attention to personality-me, that uptight-me. It looks at personality-me as if it's a poor thing, and that's all. It doesn't want to have to do anything about it, doesn't want to be kind to it. Free-me doesn't want to extend itself to that uptight creature, nor have anything to do with it. When soulful-me does get near that uptight-me, the personality grabs onto the soul and won't let it go again.

You said before that soulful-you managed to get free and move out until it ran into an obstacle. I'm still not clear what that obstacle was.

It's invisible, not really an obstacle; it's just a restriction that soulful-me experiences. When the soul becomes more aware of this restriction, it begins to look around to find the obstacle, but there just isn't any. Even so, the soul becomes immobile. Then it stops and disappears and turns into the personality again. It isn't an obstacle I can see or even sense. It's just a restriction, like someone giving me a command. It's more like a vibration I get, which isn't as profound as it used to be, and it's a little slower in getting the soul to slow down. The soul gives in because it realizes it can't win the battle. The more the soul tries to be free, the heavier the restriction from the personality. Sometimes, if the soul relaxes, it can cope with it. But eventually the personality wins. When the soul takes in more energy to get past the point of the obstacle, the personality puts out more of those resistive vibrations, going faster and faster, until it stops it. Whatever degree the soul builds to, that's the intensity to which personality-me builds up vibrations to paralyze the soul.

You say the soul wants to be free. Do you have any sense of what it's longing for in relation to this freedom it seeks?

It wants to feel comfortable wherever it is. It wants to feel satisfied, at peace. It doesn't want to have to run away from situations where it seems to have to compete, or where something is expected of the personality. The personality tries to run away from those people and situations. The soul wants to stay in those situations and still feel comfortable.

At home in the universe?

Yes. No matter where it has to go.

Allow yourself to feel the soulful, longing-for flow, in all its purity. If there's mental activity, let it float away.

Just feel the pulsing of that longing-for without attach-ment or any goal, and surrender to that. Let it expand into a oneness with this longing-for without any ideas or axe to grind, melting into that flow, separate from everything else, pure feeling-consciousness of the soul.

Personality-me stopped me. I sensed I was into the flow and personality-me jumped in and said I didn't know what I was doing. And I got pulled out of it.

Up to now, you've been telling me you haven't been able to find the time and means to practice the soul flow, even though the practice helps you. So my soul goes out to you. I accept this without question. Then you were saying that even when you're with me, you recognize some barrier that prevents your soulful flow from finding communion with my soulful flow. Now my soul is flow-ing out to you, regardless. As it's doing this, what do you sense happening within you?

Personality-me is jamming. It seems to be putting out negative vibrations again. It doesn't want my soulful-me to connect with yours.

But now there was no stopping my soulful essence from moving into her field.

I notice soulful-me has gotten into your head. It's caressing personality-you, soothing it, saying sweet things to it— like, There's nothing to be that frightened about; if you let things be, things will be better than ever.
Now it's experiencing what's in your head as a baby

needing to be caressed, needing to be loved, reassured, as that personality-you. Soulful-me is doing that now, inside your head, caressing that baby personality, loving it, holding it closely, giving it tenderness, warmth, security, fondling it like babies like to be fondled and made to feel wanted.

Personality-me just doesn't trust that.

That's OK. Soulful-me is loving that baby personality anyway, that frightened little infant.

It's not reciprocating, not trusting you, because it thinks that's one of your tricks, a way of getting at me. If it gives in, then you'll control.

Soulful-me loves personality-you in your head, regardless. It doesn't have to be trusted by it. Personality-you might even want to kick me, or bite me.

It just doesn't trust your motives. If it gives in, it would be two against one, two souls against personality-me—your soul and my soul.

Soulful-me isn't for and it isn't against. It's just there. It just is. In fact, it isn't even my soul, since it embodies all that's soulful in that flow. So it's nothing that's exclusively mine in any personal way—since I'm outside my body, since the soul is everywhere, and I'm simply being one with it.

Personality-me is saying, Well, all right! It isn't opposed to soulful-you as much. It's settling down a bit. It isn't ready to oblige, but it is ready to listen to what you have to say.

I was ready to give Lynn a guided tour of what was in my head, a sharing of what my soulful essence could read out in regard to personality manifestations. This was not only a chance for Lynn to learn more of the inner workings of my structured-self; it was a way for me to keep my interior circuits clear as well.

What soulful-me can tell it is that within my entity there is also a personality-me. If I turn myself over to experiencing its emotions, it would say pretty much the same things yours is saying. The moment I submit to personality-me I feel I'm on my own, it's individual-me in relation to the whole world. I've got to overcome all the supposed obstacles, fight illusionary battles, prove that I'm worth something, make it in competition, rounds of struggling and suffering. So my personality-me is in the same position as yours if I slip into that plane of thinking. But as soon as I step out and away from that and allow myself to be free to experience the soul in harmony with it all, then I feel the sense of universal purity, a feeling of oneness. Then being takes on a whole new tone of radiance in being fused to it all. Maybe to find out more we could let our personality-selves talk to each other along with our souls.

A four-way conversation?

It could go a whole bunch of ways.

The more you've been talking, the more my body

feels different. When you started talking and convincing personality-me, my feet began to feel heavy. Now the flow has moved up my legs, to the pelvic area. It's like I'm a worm cut in half. From the pelvis up, it won't give up.

From your pelvic area up, personality-you won't give in; but the lower part, from the pelvis down, has collapsed— is that it?

Yes. Tell personality-me again what you were trying to make my soul do.

No! If I try to reach you in some way, that's personality-me trying to work on you. If I'm one with my soulfulness, and one with the soulfulness that exists everywhere, then I'm no longer that personality-me. I have no need to try to work on anything or anyone. I've surrendered myself, beyond personality-me; I've given myself over to a pure feeling of longing for that soulfulness which, when I give in to it, begins to flow through me. To realize that soulfulness, I have to long for it without anything or anyone in terms of a demand. When I'm in that plane of longing for soulfulness, and it's flowing in me, with me and through me, then I'm no longer in control as personality-me. I'm allowing something bigger, something beyond me to take over, giving up personality-me as a limited, dependent source and shifting my reliance to a universal life-force.
When I'm there, there's only love for whatever is going on in your head. Since personality-me is not involved, my reactions flow from the transpersonal. I'm tapping into a perfect feeling realm, a love flow which is pure, clear,

infinite—a serene longing-for field of essence. It's pure sensation, nothing else. What soulful-me is now experiencing in your head is kissing all the different points of pain in personality-you—one place, another place, where there has been pain, loving and kissing all those different places.

In my head?

In your head. Caressing all the fears, the feelings of guilt, all the torment about having to be this or that bouncing around in your head. I might add that personality-me has no control over what I'm saying because of the surrender to soulful-me, which is beyond my individual entity. I'm simply letting it do what it will. That's the way the universal soul works with its infinite power, infinite love and infinite feeling.

There was a silence of several minutes.

I can see and feel you inside my head. You look just the way you do now, but I look like my daughter when she was very little with her curly hair. It looks like her, but it's me. I'm on your lap and my hair is all wet from crying while you pet me. I was crying and clinging to you and now I've stopped crying. Now I see myself getting bigger and now I'm grown up. We are just there, and you're still sitting and I'm standing. Somehow I don't feel the way I did before—still a little bit, perhaps—when you were patting me in my head, soothing the ideas I have had of not measuring up in lots of ways— the way I've been with my children, not mattering

if they're one way or another, but loving them anyway. But I still don't feel that good about myself
even though you love me despite all my faults.

I'm still inside your head with soulful-me.

Yes, but you're there in a different way now: sort
of an image, transparent, like molecules which I
know are you. I don't feel myself being caressed,
but I see you doing it.

*As soulful-me is inside your head, soulful-me is also
inside my head and loving whatever is going on inside
my head, with my heartfelt pulsings going out and into it.
So if something starts to gyrate in my head coming from
personality-me, soulful-me is able to be there in my head,
expressing its compassion for whatever personality-me
might get worked up about, cooling and soothing it, too—
very much in keeping with what it was doing in your head.*

I see personality-me in my head, the size I am now,
all teary-eyed—not so much now—and soulful-me
went up into my head too, quite easily, in the form
of a vapor flowing up from my feet, completely
enveloping personality-me. Now personality-me
and soulful-me are embracing each other. Soulful-me is now patting and loving the personality.
The personality is hugging back—not so much in
a grasping way, but more in a friendly manner,
just taking the loving from soulful-me and enjoying
it. And they are together. They're separate and also
together, sort of passing in, out, and around each
other, and personality-me lets soulful-me do it.

Before, personality-me had the urge to have your soulful-you get inside my head and caress personality-me in my head. I said before that the personality-me always has an axe to grind, always wants something, always desires something. So you see, personality-me in my head is the same way. Also as I'm saying it to you, soulful-me is saying to personality-me, But I'm inside your head; I love you, I feel you.

Personality-you wants more than that.

That's the personality. It always wants, wants, wants— particularly what is supposedly beyond its reach. I had a flash that our souls were together for a moment and our personality-selves were together as well.

They were. I think it was the same instant. I felt that the four of them were together too, not for the first time—because there have been times when our spirits have seen each other in each other's eyes—but this time it was like there was a party going on in your head. Everybody was there. The four of us were all very friendly and happy and lighthearted. Now I'm standing on level ground and looking down. Your feet go down millions and millions of miles, your legs are endless into a pinhole pit. I'm still on ground level with your chest. I'm tiny looking at your chest. I'm just a pinpoint in relation to you. The rest of you goes up out of sight—but not really out of sight. Almost. I can see you, but you're millions of miles high as I see both up and down. My spirit is still someplace in your head. I don't feel any uncomfortableness about it.

Before, I had the picture of the four entities hugging and becoming one, our personalities and souls all melting as one.

Yes! In your head. That's where I experienced it. Now your form is changing. My spirit is still in your head—no, it isn't.

I'm getting a bit tired. I've had a long day. I wanted to share that with you.

Something happened just as you were saying that. Like it ended. My spirit rose out of your head, but your whole form began to have rays coming out of it, like looking at something through some kind of prism. The colors of your trousers, your jacket, started going out in radiant points. Not shiny rays like the sun, but pointed rays—and they began to dissolve, going into the ground and all around. My spirit drifted out like smoke and went off into the air too.

I suddenly had the sense of being everywhere with you and knew it all with you.

I think your sparks were like those rays I had for myself at the very end, as if you were part of everything I know. It was almost as if you were the sun, bright and shining. Your body began to have rays coming out from the deepest pit to the sky. The rays got wider and wider, deeper, farther out, very fast. Then the rays became so big and wide that they dissolved and diffused. But at the same time, it was as if my spirit, that vapor that I saw as me, flowed in and out of your particles. Both of us just dispersed together, like we were infinitely together and then dissolved, and that's where it ended.

Lynn was all smiles when she left.

Sorting out my feelings after this session with Lynn was very difficult; however, there was one overriding tone—a heightened excitation. It finally dawned on me that I was aroused, very much as I had been back in high school when a flirtatious girl would set off waves of stimulation within me that might last for days. But what I had experienced with Lynn was beyond the sensory, sensual and sexual mode. Apparently I was dealing with another kind of pleasure, one that stirred a partial soul-to-soul interplay. I wanted to expand on that—to know the ultimate, cosmic merging of essences.
I suspected that spirit might have been offering me a further clue to infinite love, a means of flowering an infinite self, capable of realizing an infinite solution. I was prepared to enlarge my vision, but I would need to search out my hidden yearnings. Such a frame of feeling may help you to understand why Jeanine played so important a part in the evolving work.

J eanine had come to see me for the first time six months before my last meeting with Lynn, so she was what could be called a new patient. I had had the advantage of drawing on all the experiences I have related so far. Starting with Jeanine was like starting fresh, therefore, with much more background of spirit trustfulness.

The outstanding impression I had of Jeanine after our first meeting was that I was left with very little impression of her. It was her intent to make a good impression on people. Her effort wasn't aggressive, nor did it spring from a desire to appear glamorous. Rather, it was an attempt to overcome the disapproval she anticipated, which was directly tied to negative ideas she had about her appearance. She was consumed with the notion that she was a package, a commodity to be valued or not valued in the personality marketplace. She carried this attitude to the extreme, and her failure to convince others to think well of her product invariably ended in depression, the emptiness of feeling nothing. When Jeanine showed up for her first appointment, she was abjectly disconsolate and overcome by personal guilt. But the Jeanine I experienced was beyond her person. My essence was seeking some kind of contactual flow with her inner spirit source.

By this time, I had come to trust essence enough to allow it to act, so my reaction to her depression and bondage was quite different from what it might have been some time before. She was undoubtedly used to people sympathizing with her to the extent that they were afraid to offend her. But since I did not consider personality-her to be the true Jeanine, I had no problem about stepping on her psyche. My attitude flowed from essence feeling. I could intuit the pure soul within her, the hidden reservoir where a divine center dwelled. Therefore, even though she was quite inhibited, shy and controlled, I didn't have to be that way. Having essence freedom made it possible for me to remain in motion, separate from the gumminess of her perpetual self-defeatism.

In that first meeting I was not about to pussyfoot with her, nor was I driven to overwhelm her. I was merely honest, direct, and open as to the nature of her problem. In so many words, I described her as being in a squirrel's cage; said that she was stuck, not going anywhere except around and around; and that if she was to get out of that cage, she would have to want that more than anything else. I'm sure no one had ever told her this fundamental truth before. Essence told me that honesty would not shatter her, that brittleness was only her personality facade. Of course I could have waited and tried to protect her; she undoubtedly had become accustomed to such responses from other people in her life. But I just didn't function that way any longer. That was the way our first meeting ended. As a matter of fact, I discouraged arranging another appointment. I didn't want her planning to see me again merely to please me—and then, having pleased me rather than herself, not having the will to follow through. When she left, she was more shaken than when she came, but she knew more of what was possible. I had told her, also very directly, that I was helpless to help her in the way she was trying to help herself; but I was certainly not helpless to help the spirit-Jeanine that she had never allowed herself to get to know.

Four days later she called me. She asked in a quivering voice if she could see me, as if she expected me to refuse. When my essence responded with soulfulness, she seemed startled but greatly relieved. We began to work together.

Jeanine came to see me once a week for the next four months. My involvement with her was as intense as possible from the start, given her limitations. From the beginning, soulful-me was reaching for the pure source within her. Her structured-self kept sending out distress signals whenever there was the possibility of her losing herself in the pure feeling flow. At that time, none of the work included any direct spirit penetration into the deeper realms of her being because whenever I would introduce, and invite her to live out, the spirit flow she would immediately experience dizziness. It was a subtle suggestion for me to stop but I didn't, except to allow her to sort of catch her breath. This moved her tolerance of the structureless essence flow further along each time until gradually there was less dizziness and more relatedness to the spirit plane. When she decided to stop seeing me for awhile, she had had her purest session up to that point.

There were also intimations that Jeanine felt affection for me, which was difficult for her. She had struggled with an unhappy marriage which had ended in divorce a year before. Since then she had cut herself off from social contact with men.

I considered her taking her leave from me to be a healthy sign. By this time, periodic absences had become commonplace for my patients. She seemed to want to experiment with the apparent growth she had realized in her four months of work with me, and to integrate the limited spirit saturation she had absorbed.

I would be remiss if I did not mention other subtle and esoteric forces that played a part in her stopping temporarily at that time. In a sense, I was making love to her—not in the usual manner of personal seduction and conquest, but in developing a background of pure soul-mating. What was involved was a crossing—for both of us—from the personal to the transpersonal realm, where sex is functionally nonexistent: a crossing into the unified cosmic spirit flow where there is none of the individuation on which such vehicular forms as sex are predicated. Her complete surrender to the pure love flow played a vital part in all this.

I had asked her very early in our work about fantasies which set off positive feeling responses for her. She immediately mentioned two types of experience. Falling in love came first. She wanted to know a love which was, in a sense, out of this world—to feel it in such a special way with someone that it became, as she said, Bigger than both of us. Significantly, that was the very direction in which I hoped to take her—to fall into love, to the source of love energy, but a love energy flow which was universal, beyond the personal realm. Her second wish for personal satisfaction was equally revealing.

There have been times on the beach—I can remember being alone, stretched out on the clean, white sand, with nothing but the sun, the ocean, the breeze, the birds to keep me company, just letting myself soak up the warmth of the sun and the other elements. It was wonderful!

Essence was telling me of her latent readiness to know saturation by warming life-forces; giving her a gradual infusion of soulful energy was a viable direction for her.

When Jeanine returned three months later, after our preliminary work together, I knew she was ready for total penetration of soulful essence into her soul. I was ready. Whatever symptoms or difficulties she had encountered during her three-month absence had little significance to me. My soulful essence had no qualms about going beyond the bounds of what happened with Lynn, letting spirit energy plunge as far and as deeply as it wished in reaching a fusion with her soulful core. No blocks, no barriers would stand in the way of total penetration. It would be pure flow homing in on pure flow, divine intercourse. When Jeanine first sat down she asked for reassurance—as if she should have managed better on her own.

Are you surprised I'm here?

Should I be?

I quit my job since seeing you. I've been looking

for another, but nothing has turned up. I thought I'd try being freer of that, being more on my own, getting out and learning things. The job kept me tied down to the kind of work I haven't enjoyed. But I got myself into a situation. I'm back where I was when I first came to see you, in a way.

She laughed nervously.

How do you mean—situation?

I'm going with a man—it's put me in a depression. I didn't really want to go out with him, but I thought I should start socializing. He's very nice. The only problem is he wants to get involved right away. I want to take it slow, where we'd go out together as friends. He makes me feel he desperately needs me. I tend to go along with that. I feel sorry for him. Now I don't know what to do. It's as if I'm into something I won't be able to get out of—that kind of attachment. The other night I got quite depressed over it and told him I didn't want to see him anymore. Then I felt guilty and called him back the next day. I sense I might be pushing for too much too soon.

Too much too soon?

I wanted to talk to you, to find out more about this. I began to sense I was trying to figure out life, trying to think my way through it. Lately I've been doing so much thinking that I'm getting myself right back into the same condition I was in when I first came to see you.

Would it surprise you if I told you I'm treating what you're saying as a consequence of where you're at?

No.

If you're not free within yourself, the lack of inner freedom will cause you to get caught up in the sorts of things you are mentioning.

I was testing the waters, of course, prepared to ignore what was going on in her personal and social life, and readying myself to plunge into a fathomless inner incursion—and that was what I told her.

Yes! Yes! I would really like to know what I feel inside. All that outside stuff sets off my brain and gets me more and more involved with upsetting thoughts.

I wanted to settle into some kind of essence interlock with her first at least as a reference point. I took her out of her personal-self and brought her back into the pure flow.

Now, what do you sense?

It's very peaceful. I'm going deeper and deeper. The deeper I go the more peaceful it is.

I was now allowing this descending movement into my own feeling field. As I did so, there was a welling up of energy the kind of pure force which was now quite familiar to me.

I'm having a very strong overflow coming through me. It's coming from that virgin, clear, pure level, as I go back beyond that quiet space within me. It wants to move into that peaceful space of yours and give it some of that power, that pure life-force.

The impulse to let go of the soulful energy was now acting itself out.

There's some kind of force I feel rushing into me.

Can you let it pour in, accept and receive it?

Mm-hmm.

Let it rush in full-force if you can—really let that power penetrate into the depths of your space, as far as it will take itself within you, all the way in, deeper and deeper.

There was a few minutes' silence, during which I had a vague feeling of having lost touch with her.

You seem to have disappeared.

I'm floating, like I'm not even in my body any longer.

This was the first time an out-of-body experience had developed without my using any specific technique, and it startled me. It took a few moments for me to center myself again.

Just allow it to be what it is, where it is.

That's really weird. It no longer feels as if I'm sitting here. It's like I'm in outer space.

Just permit it.

The force coming from you has changed for me. Before it was rushing in; now it's one continuous flow.

See if you can let the soulful force coming from my field penetrate into your heart, like a rocket boring in, all the way in, as far as it can possibly go, right down into your soul. See if you can allow your soulfulness to receive those energy waves, to the ultimate of impregnation. Let yourself absorb it, permit the force to do what it wants upon entry, to take over, while you yield.

The steady flow has intensified. All those problems I had and felt when I came in today—they're gone. My inner self has intensified; in some way it has overcome all those problems.

How do you experience my opening your life-force to my life-force, your soul to my soul, penetrating and impregnating you, driving in with that feeling stream, as far as it can go?

It feels beautiful!

I now knew she had been reached. The direct hit was also opening up her essence to a dispersion and diffusion of soulful experiencing—a melting of soulful energies, mine and hers. As this spanning took hold, the process of liquification began to open worlds within worlds of soulfulness, moving from remnants of intellect to pure love energy. Also, I was surrendering any remaining images of masculinity to a larger realm of pure feeling—crossing to divine union, where love was pure sweetness without differentiation.

See if you can abandon yourself to my soulful flow, let it unknot all the clamps within you, loosening the spots of tension, letting them be loved, smoothing out all the rough and taut edges, feeling the softness and tenderness that comes. Now let my soulful flow move down into you, into the interior of your body, your deepest sense of being, flooding you with pure soulfulness. Let yourself feel the feelings of being loved on the inside, just like you were being made love to, soul to soul, every cell, inside your whole being, yielding, taking in more and more, soaking it up, flooding you.

This is so beautiful; I don't want to lose it. I don't want to come out of it. That flow was into every part of me; it was all over my being—so complete.

My attention shifted. I was ready to receive any soulful force that could flow from her field into mine. When I mentioned this, her energy shifted too, but in a way I hadn't expected.

The life-force feels overpowering, but I can't let it go.

Is something holding it back?

Yes! It seems to be easier for me to take—not so easy for me to give back. I'm getting dizzy again.

Apparently her structured-self was attempting to abort any loosening of her own soulful flow, repressing the love energy building within her.

Just tell yourself, She's getting dizzy, while you observe the dizziness going on from outside, from within the soulful space—meaning that personality-you is getting dizzy, while you remain free of her and don't feel dizzy.

Your life-force is overpowering me to the point that personality-me can't deal with it. Your life-force is more powerful than personality-me.

What my soulful life-force was feeling at that moment was love for her soul. It became clearer that what I was loving was not only her soul but all souls; I was seeking union with all souls to realize the ultimate bliss of oneness.

Right now my soul is feeling love towards your soul.

I guess my soul must have loved your soul, too.

Must have?

I love you!

She laughed and giggled.

Your soul loves my soul?

Right! It's hard for me to say it.

Let your soul say it. Personality-you doesn't have to be involved.

It feels it; but it also feels it's easier for me to take than to give. Right now it feels there's a kind of exchange going on, a back-and-forth kind of thing.

Let the energies, yours and mine, exchange; let them mix and run together; breathe the exchange, the sense of oneness, the closeness, intimacy, openness, blissfulness. Let it all come together.

I can't feel this with anybody else.

It seems difficult for you to let out this soulfulness within you, the love flow, even with me. Behind your facade, you have all that flowing within you. Nobody gets a chance to experience that wonder passing within you, gets to know soulful-you within—except me perhaps, and then only to a limited degree.

I guess I'm not being that self ordinarily, not that true self. But right now, I'm recharged, really recharged!

She laughed more freely.

Now I can go out and give it to somebody else.

Like a chain-letter?

Yes! You know, I don't think of you as a doctor anymore. You're somebody I can talk to; there's a special feeling I have with you that I don't have with anybody else. I'll call you Carl from now on.

Jeanine was giggling and laughing as she left. I recalled a poem I had read:

Fear not to give, in thought 'twill go in vain,
What springs eternal give, get back in rain;
But fear to keep, for stagnant pools turn stale,
And streams, because they flow, clear and rich remain.

We had experienced a state of relatedness beyond sexualism, sexual roles, sexual intimacy; I knew the infusion of spirit energy that had awakened her soulful-self would encourage her to search for even more transpersonal flow.

F reedom is relative only in personal terms; in the spirit realm it is absolute, total. So when Wayne called me a few days later, I was still in the free motion that carried over from Jeanine. He immediately put that flowing consciousness in jeopardy when I saw him.

I was trying to think of ways I could express my-self, why I've come back to see you, and the diffi-culties I'm having presently. Last night I was sitting by the fireplace. I felt this need to get into myself, into more awareness. One of the reasons may be that I don't drink anymore. My habits have changed. Before I was running around doing this or that. If I got blue, I'd tie one on. I'm too aware of things now for that. I can't turn back to those old fantasies to avoid knowing the truth—taking trips to Florida, Bermuda, to run away from myself, all that mental masturbation. That just doesn't work anymore. Apparently I've gone to a certain stage and I'm now at a plateau. So there's a gap there, a lack of a bridge to something more. Not being able to cop out has kept me in a state of not feeling well, and I'm taking the brunt of all the tensions that I thought I could put elsewhere. I

can't seem to take that step into something more. I
don't even know what to call it or how to define
it. I seem to have been going along at a certain rate.
Naturally, I'm changing in my ways, in my thinking; I'm still growing. With other people, I seem to
know just where it's at. I'm able to see through their
nonsense. I'm not upset by their behavior and can
usually detect their motives. It's a vibrational thing
I sense. But I still haven't found that one step for
myself.

Pure communion with Wayne was the inevitable next
step for establishing greater essence flow. But structured-me repeatedly argued how absurd it was to think
of dissolving into union with him.
*How are you going to find spiritual oneness with a speed
demon, someone who acts out, whose life has centered around
racing cars, airplanes, motorcycles, women, and boozing it
up? You're so different—quiet, reserved, introspective. You're
exact opposites.*
I searched for a point of crossing. I'd been wrestling
with the policy of taking fees from patients for some
time, and now the issue had come to a head. Essence
had a longing to be free and clear of that last tie to
professional-me. There was something wrong with my
taking money from Wayne if I was to realize the depths
of spirit communion with him. I had to get beyond the
cult of professionalism—the illusion of status and the
idea that there was something sacred about personal-
me. Of course, the harassment itensified.
*Do you realize what you're asking for, giving away your
services for nothing? How are you going to make a living?*

There was the strong possibility that such a move might result in more than I had bargained for. With the end of the doctor-patient arrangement, there could be no turning back.

But I had no choice. Now there was no longer any thought of being with Wayne in a certain way; just being with him would be enough and would be right as far as essence was concerned. It was so simple.

When I suggested an end to the fee at our next session, Wayne was dumbfounded. Nevertheless, he was open to trying it, as he had been with other things. I suggested we place ourselves in a neutral space. We would allow all things, such as mental thought, emotional reactions, noise or any other facet of sensory life to come and go, giving no greater value or attention to any one manifestation over another. In a way, it was technique without technique, preference without preference. There was also the hope that freeing ourselves from goals, with nothing to accomplish, would make possible a fuller immersion in the timeless, eternal now, the feeling flow of essence. It was a way of locating ourselves at an optimum point of communion despite our diverse predilections. We were silent for about twenty-five minutes.

I was going to ask you whether you were listening to the wind outside. I haven't heard it howl like that in a long time. There were certain things that crossed my mind—a strong sensation that you were thinking the same thing. The sense of that came back three or four times, of you vibrating on the same plane. At other times I felt I was on an old sailing frigate with full sails. Waves were crashing over the hull in heavy seas. It was a very strong picture, as if I had really been there.

When you had these impressions, did you just let them float by, not treating them as being more important than anything else?

Yes, but they still came back several times. There was a kind of an exuberance in being there.

See if you can return to the now without preference.

I have a feeling of being the flow. There's a connected flow between us. It has a very, very quiet spot to it, too. It's the quiet spot that's relating to you right now—even though I'm talking. I'm speaking but the actual communication is the flow. The words are unimportant. There's no element of superior or subordinate stature between us at all. This has been a problem in the past, as you know. Right now I'm feeling the flow to a greater extent with you than ever before. It's probably because I don't have any sense of difference between us. We're on an even level. Neither one of us is involved. It's this oneness flow, a universal vibration.

I suddenly experienced a deeply placed, blue-tinted space within him and a comparable space within me. The spaces were opening up.

There is definitely no feeling in relation to you as

an entity, or your entity as a man, or the image. There is a complete sense of harmony—no part of me, the man-me, no particular image of myself, either.

At that point I was overwhelmed by essence power, a driving thrust, greater than I had ever experienced. It was aimed directly at Wayne. I just gave in to it, an enormous bolt of energy, barreling through to the depths of his being, decimating any remnants of manifestation that stood in the way of a merging of the two spaces. The power force drove into him as deeply as it could—to infinity—then broadened out, allowing the spaces to resonate and converge in a total exchange. He shuddered and had to stabilize himself. He could take it all in but it still required him to make some adjustment. Then he went into an equilibrium—I'd call it a hovering position. I was in a perfect point of reference to his—so absolute, so one with his it was uncanny. There was no motion whatsoever, just a perfect attunement as the spaces found commonality. He broke the silence.

I have this funny feeling of getting hungry. Are you hungry?

No, I'm not.

You're not hungry?

He laughed.

I guess I left your belly wide open.

Yes. The flow is still there. I realize that we'd been working in an outward-bound direction. At least that was the way I was into the flow. Then we started working on an inward approach—which has been good. Right now, it's in between outward and inward. It's as if my soul and body are blending within me, with yours, with the universal oneness, similar to the wind and the trees moving outside, like the tides. It isn't that I'm going out with the flow to relieve some tension or pressure within me. It's more that I'm bringing the universe in to me, with an even flow, just like the flow of the wind, the tides, the trees moving in all kinds of ways. It's like that with us, too, that back-and-forth flow. At the moment there's no limit to my feeling.

I began to experience a destruction of images I still associated with myself. It was like seeing a mirror disintegrate. I no longer knew who I was. Then I became Wayne. I had been dissolved in front of him—and I told him so. He quickly replied.

There's no identity for me either, for either one of us. It's never happened with anybody before—ever— to have that flow, with no identity. Ordinarily there's a wall there for me.

Even as you were saying it, I wasn't hearing it. I was hearing the sound, but I wasn't hearing it. Being in the eternal now, it was just noise floating by. Not that it doesn't have any relevance, but only to the intellect, since I no longer have any sense that one manifestation is any more important than another. As I continue to feel that eternal flow with you, it's totally free.

I've been feeling the reality of that now for the first time too, really feeling it even though I'm still talking about it.

With our individualities dissolved, we were in oneness, in perfect communion without partiality. We were now one space of pure light, of pure essence. We spent the remainder of the time in silence.

Wayne began our next meeting with concerns he had regarding some important changes in his career. I was inwardly curious about the extent this would interfere with his just being with me, whether he might want to turn back the clock and expect me to relate to him as the doctor again.

I sold the aircraft Sunday. I'm getting out of the arrangement I've had with the backers; I'm in the process of dividing up the pot, and there are some bad vibes going on in relation to that. I've been wrestling with this the past few days, and also with a prospective job that appears in the offing. I'm somewhat unsettled in regard to what's going to come of this. I'm trying to feel it out, to slow it down a bit, to put things in perspective. I find myself racing a bit, trying to mentally put all this stuff in order. At times the stress builds up; then I get into myself, and I begin to realize that it isn't in the cards that things should be solved when I think they should. Funny, I can now look at it and realize how that part of me wants to push and get it all worked out—in a nice, neatly tied package.

But it really has no reality. That part of me tries to justify it by saying that the aircraft money needs to be distributed to the stockholders and to me as soon as possible. But I know it can wait. Still, I've had to take a hard stand with the backers. And I don't like that anymore. It's just not my bag to have to get into legal hassles and a tug-of-war over that. There's the idea running around in my head, of course, that if I get rid of these problems, then I also dispose of the mental activity that's pushing at me. But I'm aware of what it means, and I'm trying to maintain that core of balance that I experienced with you last time. If the mental activity starts to take over, I can pull back into my center. I'm into that center more and more times during the day. In pulling back, I also get a more realistic picture of what's happening. So the mental activity isn't able to bother me that much, not like I would have ordinarily expected. I don't feel I'm having any problems at the moment—being tied to this or that. I'm completely separate from those things as I sit here now. As far as you and I are concerned, I don't feel that what I've been telling you interferes with what's going on between us. These are just some of the loose ends I'm faced with taking care of, no more than my taking care of my personal hygiene.

I told Wayne I had spontaneously found myself just being with him while he was talking.

I located myself there, too, even before you mentioned it. I'm feeling that there's really only one source of beingness between us, this power, or whatever. If I really get down into the essence of it, I can only explain it as a universal source, more spiritual. If I really look at it, all the way into me, there's really no difference between your source and my source. They're just one. It makes sense if you admit to everything coming from the same source. As I look at it, going to the source, to infinity inside, is just the same as infinity in projecting out. I can go in, or I can go out. It doesn't seem to matter. Either way I don't come to the bottom of the well. It just goes on indefinitely.

My curiosity was straining to know more, and I started asking questions, but Wayne suddenly became perturbed.

We're starting to analyze it; we're getting into programming it. I don't know if you feel or felt that. But a couple of minutes ago, I began to withdraw and isolate myself—getting away from being with your essence. Getting into those questions may have done it, more of a doctor-patient thing. I caught that a couple of minutes ago. I started getting those vibes and began to switch off to a more independent state. I'm calling it as I see it, exactly as I see it.

He was right. Not only that, but he was getting me back on course. So I simply submitted to the life-force of his essence, surrendering to the energy coming from his field.

Now we're back in the flow again, with only one

essence going on. We're not getting into anything specific, like the questions you asked me before. I seemed to have gained something from this. Looking back over the years I've been seeing you, there's something I see for the first time. I feel it, too. I can relate it to involvements in other activities. Words have a tendency to put the flow in a frame. Do you know what I mean? There's really only one essence. It's not possible to have two essences. There is only one powerful flow. When I try to word it, something gets lost in the translation. I can't get to any definition of it, obviously. I don't see you as a person now, or an individual, or a mind. I experience us in a complete vacuum, a large, universal scale of flow. I know that for this to happen we had to dissolve our mental activity—right now we don't have any flak like that. I can talk about it and still stay in the flow. That's unusual for me. In the past, if I would start to talk, I'd immediately put programs onto things. I'm not doing that now. We're carrying on a conversation, and I'm not categorizing. I'm still able to retain the deep flow even though I'm talking. Actually, what I'm doing is experimenting with this ability, playing games with it, seeing where it can go.

I just had the picture of being able to flop down on the floor. I could go to sleep while you kept doing what you are doing; you wouldn't need me there, in the old way.

That's just what I feel, exactly how I feel. There's such a deep-rooted flow going on that the essence is all that's needed. I don't think of it as being me, though. That's what you've said about it—in the past, about yourself. I've picked it up from you, apparently. But this is also a dangerous level to get into. When I'm there, there's this emerging knowledge and understanding; it's unreal. It's not even us; it doesn't have anything at all to do with us; just that the flow is boundless, coming from deep inside me. Do you know what I'm trying to say? I think you feel it, so there's no need to say anything. I can feel your vibes; you know where it's at. It isn't possible to explain it to anybody, anyway. It's something you have to live with. I feel free talking about anything.

Yesterday, some people came to the house. I was home alone. They knocked on the door. There was this guy and a girl. There was something remark-able about her; maybe she was touched in some way by her religious faith. I invited them in. It was raining outside. They were into this religious thing, and there was a discussion for over an hour. I found it very relaxing. I went into my essence flow. They were putting all their faith in a book. They'd go back to the scriptures and say something, and I'd get back into the universal essence. I'd say to them, I don't really feel with that. I was struck by their finding such strength in the words of the book. I told them I was into more of this universal thing. She immediately said I was into the Eastern bit. I said, No, not really! They seemed a bit puzzled by me. So I told them that everyone has their own thing they turn to, that I had found mine, a certain inner peace. I told them I'd been working with someone for awhile on this.

No doubt, this essence and free spirit within me was in conflict with some of the religious things I went through when I was young. I feel free now because I don't have to cater to that stuff any longer. I look at things the way things are and feel free to take it or leave it. But as a child, with people imposing this hell-and-damnation on me, it's obvious how that was against the whole nature of the essence and pure state we're in now. It was painful then, not being able to do anything about it, not being able to decipher what was happening, or to have the freedom or wisdom that essence has given me. It had to leave me feeling stuck. I can see now how I reacted to various things in life as a result of it. But I don't harbor any ill will as a result of it. It's just something that transpired. I thought I might not have gotten over hurting about it. Evidently, it doesn't matter anymore. So there's no animosity. I couldn't conjure it up even if I wanted to. But I do feel a certain pity, and a bit of pain and sadness, for people who are stuck there. So many of them are stuck with the religious doctrines. I guess I could be classified as an atheist for saying that. But when I'm this essence—well, it's so advanced. That institutional religion is what's truly primitive. I can joke about it; but maybe it isn't a joke. But this is the way religious experience should be, this essence. This is the way it really is, anyway—this flow, this feeling between people. Which brings me to saying that I'm a little bit worried about your monetary needs. I do realize that your seeing me without the fee is the way to go, the future of a person's growth, for humanitarian reasons.

It's meant a lot for me to have given up taking money from you. I was also feeling a oneness with your impulse to give in some way, which I sense. It doesn't necessarily follow that your giving has to be to me; it can be giving to someone else—as long as it springs from your essence, as long as it is that kind of giving. If you give from that source, you may find it's very much like what I've been feeling. In some strange and yet wonderful way, it comes back, maybe in some other form, some other medium of remuneration.

I feel that stronger than I ever have before because being in this flow—it's very different from looking at things materialistically. Giving and taking from the essence—things seem to take care of themselves, from the little I know. Money preoccupations do tend to keep one in a life-and-death struggle, with all the mental activity that goes with finding and having security. But I do have this strange feeling about your not being paid a fee. Yet, when I'm in this flow of essence, I can sense that just by being there I'm doing something for other people, automatically.

Giving something very basic.

That's right. And also, it's impossible for anybody to hassle or bother me when I'm in essence, because what they're into is just something on the fringe of life. I just look at these people and feel sorry for them, being bogged down. The essence is such a simple matter to understand: that there is just one essence. It's so basic and simple—not mystical. It doesn't really require a ten-year course to understand it. Once a person has arrived at this point, it's just natural, not anything anyone has to work at—and it's universal, too.

That's the source.

And I don't have to think about it. I don't have to do anything. I can look at you—but you, as you, don't have that distinct projection. It's not you-versus-me-versus-the-lamppost. That hits home, to realize that this is what I feel, which tells me about my growth, not realizing this was possible before. It's very, very powerful. However, I don't want to use that power in any devious way. A person could really get trapped with this feeling of power. I felt this quite strongly a moment ago. I suppose that's where some people go wrong.

When you leave today, I want you to do something for yourself. Be as quiet as you can, do as little talking for as many hours as possible. Stay as much with this sense of our being with each other as you can, for the remainder of the day.

I've noticed I've been into myself more than ever this past week, staying with this quietness, not wanting to do much talking. I've noticed I can be into all kinds of activity and still feel the quietness of the flow. That also is important to me.

He was now in spirit communion, wanting more of it, wanting more continuity with it. When we ended the session, Wayne wanted very much to come back and

see me again soon. He wanted to make an appointment, but I just said, Why don't you see how you feel?
I knew he would find more communion as he opened
himself more to his pure center.

Wayne had really blossomed, revealing levels of consciousness which were quite impressive. So I was particularly careful to check the contents of the tape after
our session, to make sure the recorder had functioned
properly. Everything was in order. I took special pains
to place the tape in a container and the container in
a safe place. I was tremendously relieved. It was all
there.
I was in an exuberant mood. Two days later I turned
on the recorder, intending to transcribe the material,
but the tape was blank! I tried at least twenty different
spots; I turned it over; nothing but silence. Immediately
ego began screaming:
Idiot! Idiot! You must have ruined it!
I tried to recall what might have happened, but I
couldn't clear my thoughts. I checked the tape once
again: Nothing!
It must be on some other tape, one you mis-marked!
I checked. Still nothing. I couldn't believe it.
*You've done it. You've had it. Now the book can never be
finished. Everything that mattered was on that tape!*
As I listened, a grinding and churning tension formed
in my belly. I allowed it to build to the fullest. Although the stress was increasing, so was the sense of
essence. It was the test. Apparently, it was the chance

ego had been waiting for, a final effort to win back what had been lost.

But ego was not going to overcome the developing will integrity and power of that spirit force; essence was steadily overcoming ego, and now it spoke clearly:

Order and disorder are one. All manifestation is the same. The loss of the tape is equal to its preservation in terms of the whole.

With the return of essence purity, I understood how the book might be completed even without this last tape. But something more had emerged. I was no longer attached to the disappointment—with all its suffering, inspired by ego-desire and expectations of success—of losing the actual record of the events. I was free of that, and the pure feeling flow of that freedom was more complete and indigenous to my own nature than I had ever known before.

So I typed out my feelings about what had occurred, just as you've read. I don't know why but several hours later I decided to try the tape once more. It was all there after all, and became this chapter.

Paula telephoned me a few months later to wish me a happy new year. Her mood indicated that the spirit was helping her in her adjustment. She was still quite dependent on roles and models in attempting to satisfy the mental and emotional strivings of her structured-self. I could appreciate how correct essence had been in halting our work; to have continued would have placed her in the untenable position of making a premature crossing to an advanced stage of formless functioning, no doubt beyond her present capabilities, and surely beyond the so-called certainties she sought to structure.

I felt she was reminding me she was still there, and wanted to leave open her possible return one day. I was certainly aware of her presence, even though she was where she was, and I was where I was. No doubt she needed time and room to let the spirit do its work. Whether she would ever realize a full awakening of the pure spirit source within her, however, was beyond my knowing or control.

I had one final thought: If individuals were spending months or even years at a particular point—well, that was understandable. But the pure flow of creation within them would still be ready to unfold. They might not realize it, or admit to it, but that swirling trans-personal spirit force is going on, and on, and